Moondance to Eternity

Moondance
to
Eternity

JOHN MONACO, MD

with Sheree Slone, RN

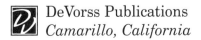 DeVorss Publications
Camarillo, California

Moondance to Eternity
© 2006 by John Monaco, MD

ISBN10: 087516806X
ISBN13: 9780875168067
Library of Congress Control Number: 2006921859

FIRST DEVORSS EDITION, 2006

DeVorss & Company, Publisher
P.O. Box 1389
Camarillo, CA 93011-1389
w w w . d e v o r s s . c o m

Printed in the United States of America

DEDICATION

To Sheree, my teacher and guide; to Mercedes, her soul;
and to Pamela, my reluctant muse.

ACKNOWLEDGEMENTS

I wish to thank all those whose contributions to this work made it possible. Gary Peattie at DeVorss and Anita Rehker deserve particular recognition. And Barbara Casey is simply an amazing agent. Without question, my gratitude for providing me with the very soul of this book goes to Sheree Slone without whom the concept would not have been born. From the wisdom and inspiration of her amazing family, incredible friends and teachers, she illuminated my life by providing me with the guidance that was essential for my spiritual growth as a human, and the spark that ignited a passion to share my experiences as a doctor in this book. Lastly, I thank my family and colleagues who have put up with my chasing a dream, much of which is embodied in these pages.

AUTHOR'S NOTE

This is a true story. As in many works of nonfiction, the stories presented are dependent upon the limitations of the author's memory. The names of certain patients, family members and institutions herein have been changed in order to protect their privacy. Also, in the interest of confidentiality, certain medical facts have been altered, but not enough to change the message of the story. Some names are accurately represented out of homage to those particular individuals and institutions. They will know who they are. The emotional reactions and spiritual growth represented herein, however, are entirely accurate.

TABLE OF CONTENTS

INTRODUCTION

In the autumn of 1999, while on tour promoting *Slim and Fit Kids: Raising Healthy Children in a Fast Food World,* I was asked by a radio show host, "So, what's next for Dr. Monaco… what will your readers be seeing next from you?" Since this was my first book and my first book tour, I wasn't quite sure I actually had "readers," but for the sake of his show I chose to answer straightforwardly.

"Well, to tell you the truth," I began cautiously, "I would like to do a book about death."

Fortunately, listeners were spared from seeing the host's color drain as his facial expressions vacillated between shock, horror and disbelief. For a brief moment I thought he was going to be sick. Since *Slim and Fit Kids* is a nutrition and fitness guide for kids and their parents, I'm sure he was expecting me to say that I was working on a book related to a similar comfortable, acceptable subject.

"Oh," he replied tentatively, "I thought you might be working on something about children, like a follow-up to your first book."

"Well, actually I was talking about children, how they fearlessly face death and…" On the spot, with the prospect of a frightening discussion he wasn't prepared for, the interviewer quickly changed the subject, skillfully bringing the interview to a conclusion. I felt shortchanged. He triggered a deep place within me, an area of my consciousness where there lived an inner urgency to shine light on a subject so avoided and misunderstood. In that instant I was poised to delve more deeply into this subject, but the passion that was ignited by his question was almost as quickly extinguished.

Over the years I have relived that moment in my mind, wishing that I had been able to take advantage of the opportunity to preview my next project. I imagine that the interview might have gone something like this:

"You see, in nearly twenty years of taking care of sick children in hospitals, I have had the unique opportunity of being present at the bedsides of many dying kids, and many of those experiences have been truly miraculous, genuinely awesome." No doubt he would have been uncomfortable with the direction of the interview, not at all sure if he wanted to venture into such territory. Not put off, I would continue, hoping to allay his anxieties as I explained further: "So, I've always wanted to write about these profound experiences which few people have. It is my conviction that readers—especially parents, family members and friends—would benefit from knowing what goes on at the time of death, especially with children whom they love and care for."

"Seems to me this might be a somewhat scary subject for people," the interviewer might say. "Especially parents!"

"Well, you're right, and that's my point."

This conversation would be much more evocative and intense than discussing the dietary and exercise habits of American youth (not that the latter are not also important)! "It would be my intention to present the subject matter in such a way that it is not scary. In fact, I think it would be quite comforting and uplifting. Besides, should it actually be scary? Death is something that will happen to all of us, and, as many scriptures and spiritual teachers emphasize, is an integral part of life.

"It has been my experience that at the very moment of death—when all present have resigned themselves to the inevitable, including the dying child—there is an otherworldly peace that becomes palpable in the room, something approaching the miraculous. It is precisely that moment that I want to write about. When it arrives, kids exhibit an innate knowledge that it is okay to die, that it is safe to transition from the earthly realm into a new dimension of life. I have witnessed many children ask their parents for permission to leave, realizing that the final moment is harder for them to accept than it is for the child who is leaving! Interestingly, a number of these children were not raised with a particular religious belief, nor were some old enough to comprehend one—their inner spirit just innately knows."

But this conversation never took place, at least not on tape or camera, even though I yearned for it to. These were really the stories I wanted to tell, but they had no context, no structure, and no tangible vehicle for their expression. The vision of sharing my experiences was an ever-present, soft background hum in my mind. There were so many inspiring and faith-creating experiences I wanted to share, but I just didn't have the proper framework for telling my story. I had come so far in my own understanding of death and its place in the continuum of life that I had an overwhelming need to share this evolution for the benefit of others, especially those who are the caregivers of dying children. But without a basic structure upon which to build a meaningful book, I felt I had to postpone fulfilling my vision until something or someone came along to help make it a reality.

You see, I entered medicine with minimal first-hand knowledge of death. True, older relatives had died during my childhood, but I had mostly been excluded from those experiences. In fact, the first deceased person I ever saw was my Uncle Joe, who died when I was a senior in high school. That experience turned out to be quite surreal after having been sheltered from death for the first seventeen years of my life. It never really registered within my consciousness that he had actually transitioned and that I would never again see his physical form.

I remember being at the funeral parlor seeing Joe's body in the open casket and thinking that it didn't resemble him in the least. Looking upon what I considered an unreal representation of him made it very difficult for my adolescent mind to comprehend that he had died. And because his death was so difficult for me to fully accept, proper grieving was impossible. Yet looking around the church the day of his funeral I saw that there wasn't a dry eye within view. He had been beloved by so many. Why wasn't I feeling what they felt? Sure, I was sad and understanding at some superficial level that he would no longer be there for me. But the concept of death's finality was too abstract for me to grasp. I envied those who were able to authentically grieve that day. They seemed to understand what it all actually meant. This wonderful, former deputy chief of police of Schenectady, New York, whose funeral resembled that of a head of state with hundreds of uniformed policemen from across the state lining the streets in front of St. Helen's Church, to me was simply "gone."

To a 17-year-old baby boomer, death was utterly confusing. To deal with it, I had to compartmentalize, file the experience in a place to be accessed only if I needed it, and then with the fervent hope that it would be seldom. How naïve I was when on that poignant day I created a highly effective defense mechanism that I would access far more frequently than imaginable—both professionally and personally—when coming face-to-face with death in the years to come.

Interestingly, at about the same time that I was grappling with the reality of my deceased uncle, many young men slightly older than I were leaving for the rice paddies and killing fields of Vietnam. Did they have similar experiences with death during their childhoods, making them equally unprepared to deal with it? Were they sheltered from death in their childhood like I had been in mine? Had the bloodless gun fights on TV and the twentieth-century belief that disease could be conquered by modern medicine left them unprepared to deal with the reality, mystery, and misery of death, imagining that it might actually be preventable? Does this at least partially explain why the horrors of so much seemingly meaningless death left so many young men psychologically damaged for life?

My first experience with death of someone other than a family member came on the very first night of my pediatric residency when a patient assigned to me died. In a very direct way, this experience set the tone for the unexpected path on which my medical training and practice would take me. Ironically, I entered pediatrics because of its association with youth, life, and perceived immortality. But as a foreshadowing of things to come, and as an early wake-up call to life, death, and medicine, my first patient died. It was not until much later that I grasped the immense significance of this seemingly random event. I would never be fully trained as a physician—it became clear to me later—until I was educated in death. I would not completely embrace life as a human being until I embraced death. I would no longer fear death until I accepted it. And I could not accept it until I no longer feared it. For a first-year resident it was like a Buddhist koan—a paradoxical conundrum that later became one of the guiding truths of my life.

Solving the conundrum did not come without pain, however. Before you get the wrong idea, it wasn't as if my patients died at a higher rate than those of any other physician. But when a patient was near death, or when death was inevitable, it seemed that I was the one who was always nearby. Either I was drawn to them or they to me; I am not sure which. Even my choice of specialties, pediatric critical care medicine, put me in the Intensive Care Unit (ICU), where death is a regular occurrence. Why did I not end up in general pediatrics, which had been my original plan, where much of the day is spent with the joys of healthy newborns and mild infections? Very simply, that was not to be my journey.

The most challenging part of my awakening came with the experiences not in the hospital, but in my own personal life. Just as I became convinced that I had conquered the fear of death relative to my medical practice, tragedy hit my home and my own family and friends. None of the lessons I had learned in the hospital served me, which forced me to realize that they had not been fully integrated and therefore were not authentic, since they could not be translated to real life at the kitchen sink level.

It was only after these wake-up calls that my spiritual growth began to mature. Through the spiritual practices of study, contemplation and prayer, I came to a deeper understanding of death within the context of eternal life. After years of simply not having the time for spiritual concerns, I returned to church. I listened with new hunger to the wisdom-teachings of love, forgiveness and immortality that were spoon-fed to me as a child, and that now mandated the immediacy of practical application.

I journeyed beyond the confines of traditional Western teachings in an attempt to get spacious perspectives on spiritual matters in general, and death in particular. Several sources were essential in getting me to a place of peace and understanding, and I should mention them here: *A Course in Miracles* taught me the simple beauty of the concept that the opposite of love is fear, among many other practical lessons. James Redfield's *The Celestine Prophecy* taught me to appreciate the significance of the individuals who cross our path and how life's experiences fit together into a synchronistic mosaic of understanding. Wayne Dyer helped me to understand the interconnectedness of all creation and that closeness to God comes only with closeness to one another—to humankind. He reinforced the importance of the spiritual side of who we are and the choices we make. Deepak Chopra allowed me to better understand the spiritual aspects of humanness and how they correspond to the physical qualities of life. Further, I learned the important lesson that coincidences are messages from God that can only be heard if we choose to listen, and are made real when put into everyday practice.

I also read the works of more traditional mystical contemplatives such as Thomas Merton and C.S. Lewis, who helped me to understand the artificial demarcation between the secular and the spiritual, and that one aspect of our life cannot be lived without acknowledging its opposite. Doors began to open and finally my soul began to see the light of day. It was as if I had been denying the spiritual side of my existence, focusing my energies instead on the temporal aspect of the physical. It was encouraging to see that so many individuals down through the ages sought answers to the very questions that now plagued me. Did they find their answers? Could I, too, find peace?

During this process I rediscovered the New Testament, which had a profound impact on me. When read from the perspective of understanding death, it became clearer to me what was meant by the stories of the resurrection—the continuity of one's existence—stories that I later gained the faith to accept as reality.

Yet, even after all this, there remained uncertainties and insecurities. Certainly the great questions that have tormented mankind for centuries—questions of life and death, the soul and consciousness—could not be answered after only a few years of study. Surely there was another step in my journey. And I was still overcome with the strong desire to communicate, somehow, what I had thus far learned. In time, it became intuitively clear to me that I had to write about my direct experiences with death and what they taught me. I was always told that no one learns more about the subject he teaches than the teacher—we teach what it is we need to learn. This, then, would have to be the next step. The more I thought about it, it was not that much of a stretch for me.

I had spent my entire career comforting parents by attempting to make what seemed incomprehensible and overwhelming into something understandable and acceptable to them. This took the form of bedside conferences with patients and their families, and conferences with nurses. I was even writing a monthly column for Pediatrics for Parents, which was designed to make the complex simple. "We fear most that which we do not understand," I used to tell the parents of my critically ill patients. Death is not to be feared; yet it is death that patients, families and their physicians fear most. And it is the fear of death that guides all modern therapies. I saw tragedy not in the failure of medicine to prevent death, but rather that when death is inevitable tragedy comes in the fear we have of it, in the inability to accept it and provide comfort to those who are facing it.

Still, I had no book. All I had was a catalog of experiences and a chronology of my spiritual evolution. I could never sell that idea, significant as it was, to a publisher. I needed something more, something that tied it all together.

Then, in the spring of 2002, I had a conversation with Sheree Slone, with whom you will become acquainted later in my story. She had become a very important friend to my wife and me as we struggled with the tragedies in our own lives. To my wife, she was a spiritual guide. To me, she was nothing short of a full professor of all that is spiritual and its interrelationship with our earthly journey. Thanks to her, we survived. Thanks to her we were able to face the rest of life with joy, optimism, with our hearts at peace. Sheree was the inspiration behind much of the study I outlined earlier. There she was, right under my nose—my own personal teacher and inspiration. She, I thought, might have the answer as to how to bring this knowledge and experience together in a book.

On this particular day, however, she came to me with a request for help. She had always wanted to write a book about her own spiritual journey, which had been profound. Based on my experiences with publishing *Slim and Fit Kids,* she wondered if I might be interested in writing her experiences and, hopefully, getting them published. It was at that moment that the proverbial light went on: Why not combine our stories? Using Sheree's experiences to elucidate my own could provide me the perfect vehicle for finally delivering my message: Death is not to be feared.

Suddenly it all made sense. After all, the evolution of my understanding meant nothing without her involvement. And the story of my evolution gave her experiences substance and significance. So the partnership was born, and out of it came *Moondance to Eternity.*

The time then came to integrate these experiences into a cohesive narrative. It quickly became obvious that this work would be more than I had originally intended. It was not just about children, or even simply about dealing with death. What happened in the process of putting our experiences together is that once again—as has happened so many times in my life and career—the children had become the teachers. It was they who launched my own journey into a deeper understanding of the mystery of life, death, eternity and, even more importantly, the importance of love as the source of joy. These were lessons of import and encouragement to every potential reader—not just children, parents, or medical caregivers, but everyone.

Perhaps it is the simplicity and innocence of children that make them consummate teachers, along with their disarming lack of ego. The strength they possess, the faith they demonstrate and the courage they exemplify are examples to us all. As I contemplated further, I realized that the essential message of *Moondance to Eternity* should not be how to face death, but how to live life. And, more specifically, how in freeing ourselves from the fear of death, life may be lived to its fullest. In fact, it can and should be lived with the joyful abandon of childhood.

As you will read, on April 3, 2002, the inspiration for the book's title came to me and, four months later, so did the bulk of the manuscript which evolved into the book you now hold in your hands. It is my heartfelt wish that these pages contribute to your appreciation of the entire cycle of life with faith in its rich, mysterious beauty. At the very least, I hope you are encouraged, strengthened, and uplifted by the stories of the heroes and heroines of the book—the children who courageously demonstrate that death is not to be feared, and the miracles revealed through their example. Ultimately, I hope this book supports you in living the remainder of your life joyfully, with the knowledge and faith that death is a safe passage, and that life is an exquisite dance, a moondance to eternity.

CHAPTER ONE

Felix

Doctors hate death. I am no exception. We are, of course, trained to avoid it. We accomplish this in several ways. Obviously, we do everything medically possible to keep our patients from dying, which is our job. But when death is inevitable, when we have failed to keep death at bay, we run. It's not so much that we are afraid of death (although most of us are), it's just that we don't know how to handle it. We haven't been trained for it. In fact, death is the antithesis of everything we have been trained for as doctors. It is the most dreaded enemy whom we fear, loathe, and escape from every chance we get.

Naturally, when I began my pediatric residency in 1981, I shared the common affliction of fearing death and all that was associated with it. Facing patients for whose care I was responsible was terrifying enough. Death was the least of my worries—except my own, of course. My own survival was an essential motivator. Impressing the attending physicians—my bosses—was another. I learned very early that the best way to win them over was by imitation. So that was what I needed to do: watch them, be like them, and eventually become them.

Medicine remains—as it was during the Middle Ages—a craft learned best by apprenticeship. Many years are spent in classrooms, lecture halls and laboratories; however, the real learning takes place at the bedside. We learn how to deal with patients by watching our teachers, the senior physicians, the attendings. We make rounds with them, observing the ways in which they apply their knowledge and experience to clinical situations. We watch the way they examine patients, the way they converse with the sick and their concerned families. In pediatrics, students are particularly mindful of the way children are treated. How do the attendings interact with them? Do they treat the children with respect? Do they talk to them as little adults, or in a developmentally appropriate way?

These and other questions were on my mind, to one degree or another, as I began my first rotation on the first day of my pediatric residency in the Neonatal Intensive Care Unit. My attending, Dr. Alexander, had a kind of charisma that was intimidating. His staff adored him, the parents of his tiny premature babies revered him, and the patients—two-pound babies who couldn't breathe for themselves or maintain their own blood pressure—seemed to do whatever he expected of them. He made the rules and everybody followed, especially the residents. Dr. A was the NICU.

There were to be three residents on call for the NICU that July in 1981. As a result we would be on call every third night, overnight. By some stroke of luck that I no longer remember, I was chosen to take the first night on call. Naturally, I was terrified. I was expected to attend high-risk deliveries and resuscitate babies if necessary. I was to be prepared to admit any new babies to the unit, and be the first line for any emergencies that might come up during the night. Of course there would be a senior resident on call elsewhere in the hospital if I needed him, and Dr. A was always only a phone call away. Still, I was scared to death.

The first day was a blur. Everything was new and incredibly exciting. I had been in delivery rooms in medical school, but to be actually stabilizing a baby before handing it to its mother was absolutely intoxicating. Assigning APGAR scores, placing tubes and lines if they were needed, reporting my activities to Dr. A—it was all very heady stuff. I reveled in it. It was the drama that excited me, and I couldn't get enough of it.

As I remember, there were about twenty or twenty-five babies that were inpatients in the NICU. Our first activity of the morning was to make rounds on each of them. This consisted of standing at each infant's bedside, space-age isolettes designed to provide each baby with his or her own personal environment, while the nurse reported the status of the baby as well as any events that occurred during the previous night that might affect the baby's care. Often the nursing report was redundant; however, since Dr. A was omniscient, he knew everything that happened with his babies, usually as it happened. I remember wondering if I would ever possess the mental capacity to remember so many facts about so many babies.

During morning rounds, we came upon an empty isolette, but clearly one that had only recently become vacant. The bed covers were disheveled and there was a tiny rattle near the head of the bed with the word "Felix" inscripted in dark blue letters on a light blue background. That same name was carefully hand-written on a card that had been taped to the glass covering of the isolette. There was a pacifier in the other corner—one of the hospital-issued ones—and at the foot of the bed were several inches of discarded IV tubing with a blood-clotted catheter still attached.

"Anything new?" Dr. A uncharacteristically mumbled to the nurse as we approached the abandoned isolette.

"No." Her tone was equally muted. "The mom and dad have been here all night, holding the baby. They seem OK with everything."

Dr. A simply nodded at this remark and had already begun moving to the next bed when he remembered that I had been quietly standing just behind him. "I'll tell you about Baby Gomez later. But don't worry, there's nothing to be done now." He glanced back toward the nurse while directing these words at me. I wasn't sure, but I could have sworn that the nurse had an ever-so-subtle smirk as she turned away to go back to her work.

I was momentarily confused but happy not to ingest the details of another complicated case. It occurred to me that the infant may have just died or was about to. But if Dr. A didn't want me to concern myself with such details then that was fine with me. Eventually I did hear about Baby Gomez. At the very end of afternoon sign-out rounds, when work is assigned for the night, Dr. A told me his story. It was true: Baby Gomez was dying. He was born with a condition called hypoplastic left heart syndrome, a congenital heart disease for which, in the early 1980's, there was very little that could be done. The diagnosis is usually made several days after birth when the body attempts to convert from its intra-uterine fetal circulation to the normal cardiovascular circulation.

Since there is essentially no functioning left ventricular to pump blood to the baby's body, he experiences severe shock and without dramatic intervention will die.

The Gomez parents, only in their late teens or early twenties, had been told this when Felix was already attached to full life support: a tube in his windpipe to attach him to a ventilator; IV lines protruding from his umbilical stump; monitor leads stuck to his tiny chest; temperature detectors and oxygen saturation probes stuck to his skin; blood transfusions and medicines to keep his heart pumping and his blood pressure up. They asked if any of this was doing any good. When they were told it was keeping him alive right now but would not sustain him indefinitely, and that there was no known way to fix his underlying heart problem, they asked that he be taken off the machines and be allowed to die peacefully.

For twenty-four hours baby Gomez was held in his parents' arms in the quiet of an out-of-the-way hospital room, waiting to die. Even by the time I trained, the staff realized that dying patients, even babies, needed to be with their families. This was fine with them because if there was one thing they hated it was having a dying baby hanging around the unit, a constant reminder that there were some sick newborns that they could not help. They liked to think that they could save anyone, and to a large degree they could. Baby Gomez and those like him ruined their record by reminding them that the powers of life and death were beyond their control, a thought with which the NICU staff was extremely uncomfortable.

"So I am just telling you about him so you know he's out there," Dr. A matter-of-factly mentioned as he completed his sign-out rounds with me. "You shouldn't have to really do anything, unless he codes. And remember, he is a NO CODE, so don't try to be heroic. If he dies, just let me know." And that was all he had to say about Felix Gomez. I remember hoping desperately that he would not die that night, not my first night on call. Let me deal with the live ones first, I thought. I can learn about death anytime.

Unfortunately, my prayers were not answered and little Felix died that night. It was about two o'clock in the morning, just as I thought I might escape having to face it. I remember the time because I had just looked at my watch thinking that I might get three or four hours sleep before morning rounds. It was at that moment that my pager went off.

"Baby Gomez is gone." The matter-of-fact voice at the other end was the charge night nurse who had introduced herself to me earlier. I didn't think she was a big fan of new residents.

"OK, do we need to call Dr. A?" I asked sheepishly.

"I already have. You just need to come and pronounce him." And she hung up.

I had not considered this. I knew from medical school rotations that when a patient died in the hospital someone had to pronounce that person officially dead and give a time of death for the death certificate. I just hadn't thought that responsibility would fall on me, at least not so soon! At that moment I feared facing that poor child and his family more than anything I experienced that memorable first day. What I did not count on was that pronouncing Felix Gomez and facing his parents would have an overpowering impact on me. As I sit here now, over twenty years later, I remember that night as if it were yesterday.

Hospitals take on a surreal air in the middle of the night. At times they can be foreboding, as the darkened rooms hold uncertain eventualities. Other times there can be warmth, the welcome feeling of being a guest in someone else's life, privileged to share the private moments that occur only in the depths of night.

As I walked down the hall to the Gomez's room, I did not feel foreboding. I did not feel the specter of death lurking in the shadows, as I thought I might. There was no wailing and sobbing as I rounded the corner toward their room, even as I strained to listen, fully expecting to hear it. Instead there was silence punctuated by muffled tones of conversation between people loving and comforting each other.

When I arrived at the room, the charge nurse was standing beside two young adults holding a baby. The parents (at least I assumed they were the parents since I had not yet met either baby Gomez or his mom and dad, because neither Dr. A nor I felt it necessary to talk to them until the end had arrived) were sitting close together on the edge of the bed. Mother had Felix in her lap. He was wrapped completely, leaving only his nose and eyes exposed. Father had one arm around mother, and with the other he gently stroked the top of the baby's head.

I just stood there for a moment, not knowing exactly what to do or say. Though only seconds passed, it felt like an eternity. Mother looked up at me and smiled and Dad soon followed doing the same. I was transfixed by their faces and their smiles. Why are they smiling at me, I remember thinking. I returned their smiles though far less comfortably. Several more moments passed before I remembered to take out my stethoscope and handle the matter at hand.

When the parents opened the bedclothes exposing a tiny section of the infant's chest, I slid my stethoscope on the place they had prepared for me. Our faces were extremely close together now, but

I could not make eye contact. I stared at the bell of my stethoscope. I was petrified. Would this be the kind of dramatic moment I had seen on TV and in movies where the realization hits loved ones that their family member is officially dead? Would this be the moment when they burst into tears and begin pounding on my chest, having to be restrained by the nurse?

As I rose up, I finally looked in Mother's direction. She was already looking at me. I remained speechless. She reached for my hand, gripped it firmly, and nodded. I smiled back and nodded in return. Still holding my hand, she leaned over and kissed the baby's forehead. I saw the father's body shudder for a moment as a tear dripped from his closed eye. Not a word was spoken between us in that room that night.

I had never been so torn in my life. I wanted the mother to let go of my hand so I could get out of the room and back to the land of the living, or at least to those who had a chance at living. At the same time I felt absolutely honored and privileged to be there, as if I were in the presence of a miracle, and I didn't want the moment to end.

But the moment did end and I returned to my call room for an attempt at fitful sleep, trying to make sense of what I had just been through. The next morning we began rounds and never mentioned Baby Gomez. I noticed, as we passed what had been his isolette, that it had been emptied and cleaned, and that his name card had been removed from the glass.

CHAPTER TWO

Alex

Conventional wisdom holds that doctors should not become emotionally involved with their patients. At first I had a difficult time understanding this rule. I was never smart enough to separate my emotions from my intellect, or so I thought. But my experience with Felix taught me that it was not only possible to separate science from emotion, it was essential. Something happened in that room that night that I did not understand. Whatever it was, it was not going to help me learn pediatrics. If anything, it might be a distraction. I would have to be careful, I told myself, lest I get drawn into the emotion of medicine and lose track of the science.

For the remainder of my NICU rotation I avoided dying patients. But I did so no more or less than any of the other staff. Just as I had learned with Felix, these patients were dying, and there was nothing more medically we could do to help them. Our job was done. Better to just leave them alone and let them die.

After I finished my time with the sick newborns, it was time to learn to take care of the big kids on the wards. I felt much more at home there. It was more like the real world. Kids had diseases most people had heard of like pneumonia, and asthma, and diabetes, not hyaline membrane disease or transient tachypnea of the newborn. By the time I was second year I was quite comfortable and many of the first-year residents looked to me as a teacher. It wasn't that I was anything special, this is simply the way the system itself is designed. I just seemed to be working well within the system.

Then I met Alex, another dying patient. By trying to avoid death, I seemed to be attracting it. Alex was assigned to me as I began my second-year rotation on the general pediatric ward. He was eight years old and had cystic fibrosis. I first met Alex when I inherited him as a ward patient, and later had him assigned to my clinic as a first year. It was from Alex that I learned how to care for patients with this disease. Since I had a cousin who had recently passed away after a twenty-year battle with this horribly cruel affliction, I had somewhat more than a passing interest in it.

I had the opportunity to learn first hand what a tragic disease CF is. In the early 80's, being diagnosed with CF was a death sentence. The point of treatment was to prolong a patient's life as long as possible and hopefully during that short life to provide as much quality as one could. "Quality" was then and remains now a relative term. Huge amounts of time at school were missed, and much of childhood was spent between clinic visits and hospital admittance.

CF is a genetic disease, therefore inherited, which adds to the guilt it invokes in the parents of these children. The basic defect is at the cellular level. Because of a malfunction of the sodium pumps, the body produces extremely viscous secretions. These occur in many organs of the body, but the ones most profoundly affected are the pancreas and the lungs. This results in thick lung secretions that are difficult to clear, creating a perfect medium for the development of pneumonia and other lung infections. Today, there are specific therapies directed at correcting the biochemical abnormality that creates this propensity for infection, thus preventing its occurrence. Twenty years ago all we could do was fight the infections. Antibiotics and respiratory therapy were the mainstays, and life expectancy was in the teens, while today it is well into adulthood. CF also affects other organs, resulting in a deficiency of enzymes required to break down nutrients, particularly fats. As a result, children with CF have difficulty growing and developing normally, further compounding their respiratory problems.

Alex had severe CF. At age eight his lungs were already severely damaged from years of chronic and acute infections. He was tiny, about the size of a small five-year-old, giving him an unnatural cuteness which made him a favorite with the nurses. He had jet-black hair and bright blue eyes framed by extremely long, thick eyelashes. His eyes had a sparkle of life, even when he was feeling miserable. He loved every day of his life, including the days in the hospital. The nurses and doctors were his family, his friends, and he knew more about them than they would have liked. You see, Alex was a bit of a gossip and loved to ask questions, which he did in a successfully manipulative way.

As mentioned earlier, the first day I met Alex was near the end of my first year. I was beginning a month on the general pediatric ward, and since Alex was admitted to the hospital from the ER the previous night, he was assigned to me. I walked somewhat cautiously into his room after being briefed on his multiple hospital admissions and somewhat legendary status on the ward. I shall never forget seeing him sitting there on his bed in his characteristic tripod stance, oxygen canula placed to his nose, head bobbing with the work required for each breath. An oversized NY Yankees hat sat on his head, and his stick-like arms protruded from a huge sleeveless Philadelphia 76ers jersey. He loved sports and idolized athletes. Over the years he had amassed an impressive collection of sports memorabilia from many teams.

"Good morning, Alex." I tried to be as upbeat as possible.

"Well, hello, Dr. Monaco." I had no idea he knew my name and found it a bit disconcerting. "You're one of the new guys, aren't you?"

"Well, yes, I guess so…." I could feel the beads of sweat beginning to gather on my forehead. "You know me?"

It sounded like a silly question to both of us, but he chuckled first. "I know all you guys." He went back to his coloring and watching TV (this was in the days before video games) in his curiously detached manner. "I thought you all knew this by now."

It seemed we had gotten off on the wrong foot. From the manner in which he looked away and went back to the business of his distractions, I had the distinct feeling that he was already disappointed in me, that he expected more intelligent conversation out of me, more snappy exchange.

Alex did not hold negative feelings long, however—he didn't have enough time—so eventually we bonded to the point that we looked forward to seeing each other every day. I'm not sure if it was my stories about seeing Mickey Mantle and Roger Maris when I was his age, or the fact that I didn't always discuss his illness that he appreciated. In any event, he seemed to see me as somehow different, less of a threat. I hoped it was that he saw me more as a person, which made me happy. Alex had become an ego issue for me: I wanted to be loved by this kid, this legendary patient that everyone knew but no one had won over. I took it as a personal challenge, and when it seemed that I had accomplished my goal, I was pleased to have experienced such a victory in one of the many battles that I faced during those early years. However, I had no idea at the time that this victory would come with a price.

Even though I was intellectually aware of Alex's prognosis, I don't think it truly sank in that he would soon die, that is until his dying process was upon us. It was six or seven months into my second year. Once again I was notified by the on-call resident that Alex was admitted the night before. This time, he added, he's "really sick." I wasn't worried, because I had heard this before.

After the first time I cared for him in the hospital, Alex attended my pediatric clinic. He had already been through all the older residents and had either worn them out or vice versa. In any event, he asked to attend my clinic, and since then I had cared for him through several pneumonias—some of which were managed as an outpatient and others which required hospitalization. I developed a feel for Alex's CF flare-ups. Whether in the hospital or at home, no matter how sick he seemed to be he responded very well to broad spectrum antibiotics, and usually within forty-eight hours of their initiation he was much better. This admission, however, was different.

It wasn't his terrible color or the fact that he was struggling so hard to breathe that bothered me. What was different this time was the look in his eyes. Alex's characteristic sparkle was absent. It was replaced by a sadness tinged with fear. Two other things were different: first, he wasn't wearing a baseball cap. Inside it sat, looking abandoned, on the bedside table; secondly, Alex's mother, a single mom who worked nights, was sitting on the bed beside him. Although Alex was her only child, she was also the caretaker of her sister's young children. For her, Alex's disease and even his hospital admissions had become routine. Once she brought him to the ER with an exacerbation, experience taught her that he would be admitted, and when the medicines were initiated she knew he would improve rapidly so she could return home. This time, however, she did not leave the hospital. In fact, she hardly left his bedside. She was worried, and now so was I.

In tune with his mother's premonitions, Alex did not respond to antibiotics nor respiratory therapy as he usually did. We even tried more heroic measures, like taking him to the operating room where the pulmonologist performed bronchial lavage, a procedure where thick mucus and infection are sucked out through a bronchoscope. We did this two or three times. Each time he had momentary improvement, but within twenty-four hours his lungs once again deteriorated. With each treatment he became weaker and took longer to recover. He was wasting away. Death was imminent.

Amongst the staff the usual reactions to the inevitable were beginning to take place. The ward team no longer entered Alex's room during rounds. What few words we exchanged were said in the corridor outside of his room, out of earshot. As the end drew closer there was less and less to say.

Within a couple of days of his death we didn't discuss Alex any more. We barely mentioned his name. It was still my job to take care of him, but it was understood that his case no longer contributed educationally to rounds. So Alex lost his privilege of being discussed by the staff. Not only was he abandoned, but so was I, his caregiver.

Work was still required, however. The nurses had plenty to do, perhaps even more than if Alex were improving. Alex's mother literally moved into his hospital room and the nurses did everything they could to make her comfortable. She spent much of her time crying, and there was growing concern among the nurses that Alex was comforting and taking care of her more than she was him. Social workers, clergy, and others were consulted, but Alex's mother had no use for them. She had her rosary and her Bible, and that was all she needed. Her job was to pray for a miracle, and the only miracle she would settle for was recovery, full recovery.

Meanwhile, I was torn. I had not been in the room of a dying patient since Felix Gomez died, which was over a year earlier. Not that we hadn't lost patients during that time—Lord knows we had! But I had managed to find ways to avoid the trauma. Not that I was shirking my duties, for the clinical demands of saving lives were simply too great. The fact is we were not expected to waste time with patients we couldn't save. What was the use? If they needed comforting the nurses and family were there to provide it. We doctors could not be bothered with such trivialities, the "psychosocial bullshit," as one of my colleagues so endearingly described it, of dealing with a patient who could no longer be served by the science we had to offer him.

Alex had come to expect me at his bedside—during morning and afternoon rounds—and I was simply unable to turn my back on him. I sincerely wanted to, not because I lacked compassion, but because I feared he would ask me about dying, or something equally sensitive. I was in no way equipped intellectually, emotionally, or spiritually to handle such a discussion, especially with an eight-year-old. It turned out I was far less equipped than he was.

Our visits had become more brief, but that was okay with him as long as I showed up. Even if we simply discussed the ball scores from the night before, or if I once again told him how I saw Mickey Mantle on the street in Cooperstown, he was happy. To avoid going to Alex's room like all the others did would have been too cruel, so that became my motivation for continuing to visit with him.

I remembered how it had been months earlier in baby Felix's room: that strange calm, the unspoken love in the room, the eerie peacefulness. Those feelings confused and frightened me, and I was not yet ready to face them again. So I kept my visits with Alex brief. I almost always prefaced the visit by saying that I was very busy that day with many other sick children to see. I would ask him how he felt, then put the stethoscope in my ears before he would even have the opportunity to answer. I'm sure he sensed my withdrawal. There is no doubt in my mind that he knew he was dying, even though we had not specifically discussed the matter. He may have wanted to, but I used every conversational strategy I could to avoid the subject. When I said goodbye after each visit, his smile was there, even if the sparkle in his eye had begun to fade.

Then one morning, when the end was expected at any time, I walked into Alex's room to find him in his mother's arms, in the rocking chair alongside the bed. They were rocking ever so gently. She held him to her chest like a swaddled newborn. He had lost so much of what little weight he had that he actually fit perfectly. I did a double take, not even sure at first that it was him.

The room was dark, and their image was obscured. She was crying. I realized that although she was holding him, he was actually comforting her. His hand was stroking her hair as her head rested on his shoulder. He looked up at me, a faint smile on his lips. A single tear ran down his cheek. His voice had been reduced to a whisper. "Could you put me back in bed, Dr. M?"

As I bent down to pick him up he nuzzled his head into the crook of my neck. I felt his arms tighten around my neck. I realized we had never before embraced. And at this late date, when I was simply forced to muster the courage to hold him, I was shocked. He had become a virtual skeleton, wasted by this unforgiving disease. He felt incredibly fragile, a delicately carved wooden doll who, if he was dropped, would surely shatter into a thousand pieces. I gently set him on the bed, but he would not let me go. He drew my ear to his lips and whispered almost unintelligibly, "I love you, Dr. M." I simply drew back away from him, attempted to smile but could not speak, for fear of the tears that would undoubtedly come forth.

To this day I regret that I had neither the strength nor courage to respond verbally to his admission of love. I hoped he knew that I loved him. I live with the assurance that he knew that I did, and that he was comforted by that awareness.

Alex wanted so badly to curl up on his pillow and go to sleep. He was exhausted. All he could manage, though, was the tripod position that had become his trademark. With what little strength remained in his fragile body, he reached for his Yankees cap and put it on. Turning to me, he barely smiled as I left the room.

That day, Alex's mother followed me into the corridor. She had been crying and frequently dabbed tears from the corners of her eyes. "I need to talk to you about something," she said. Alex had asked her for permission to die. No one had spoken to him about death, not even her. She told me she knew that he would probably die, but hoped it would not be so soon. "I could not give him permission," she admitted to me. It was too much for her to bear. "What do you think I should do?"

I looked her in the eye with a strength I could only have gotten from Alex himself. I told her calmly that Alex was exhausted, that his lungs were barely functioning, and he would not live much longer. I told her that he was a wonderful kid who wanted her to be okay, that he probably did not want to let himself die until he knew that she was ready.

She was not ready, she told me. I told her that she must accept that Alex had come to the end of his road. Giving him permission to die would be the ultimate act of love, and he would die knowing that she loved him. She hugged me and began to sob. As she walked back to Alex's room, I felt myself shudder.

I had no idea where my words came from. I hurriedly ran to the call room and locked the door behind me. At last I allowed myself to cry in private, knowing that Alex's mother was, at that moment, giving her only son permission to die.

I was not in the hospital the night Alex died. I successfully avoided his moment of death, much to my relief. Instead, I received a phone call at home from the resident on call. She said she knew how much Alex had meant to me, and she wanted me to know that he had passed away, and that it had been as peaceful as possible. I remember thanking her, and then half-heartedly asking her if she thought I should come in to the hospital. When she said that she didn't think that was necessary I was relieved.

Alex had grown to mean a lot to me. As for the full impact of his death upon my life, I still wasn't sure. Since I felt completely unequipped to deal with Alex's death directly, and since I wasn't required to do so, I decided to stay away from the hospital altogether. I rationalized this by telling myself that I wanted to deal with Alex's death in my own way. In truth, I simply wanted to avoid it.

I recall lying in bed that night thinking a thousand thoughts. Some were about Alex and how he must have felt during those last hours, those oxygen-starved moments before he died. But most of my thoughts, I'm ashamed to admit, were about myself. Whether I had wanted to or not, I had involved myself with a dying patient, and I had done this more than any other resident in our program. That last day or two had been terrible. I had completely underestimated how dependent upon me Alex and his mother would become as death approached. Had I gotten too close?

At the same time, because I stayed with them, maybe I actually did them some good. Lord knows, no other resident was willing to get so involved and, consequently, I was getting favorable recognition for my actions. Maybe I could do this; maybe I could be the doctor who could do it better than anyone else! I didn't want to be known as the "Doctor of the Dying," but it would certainly help my career to be perceived as the doctor who was not afraid to face death.

That night I experienced no spiritual revelations or insights after Alex died. Death was something that happened to other people, to patients. It was the end. It was over. Nobody I knew really understood it. In fact, as much death as we saw during residency training, we never discussed what it really meant to us personally.

It became clear that if I was going to take care of sick kids I might as well face the fact that death was in my future, and that there wasn't much point in continuing to avoid it. Never did I consider death to be in my own future, mind you—at least not for a very long time. Yet it would be in the futures of my patients and, in some cases, the immediate future.

Alex's death did represent a turning point for me. I was intimately involved with a dying patient and survived it. Not only that, I improved my own reputation as a compassionate physician by participating so closely in his death. Perhaps this was a bit selfish, but what did it matter as long as the patients benefited somehow from my new approach? From that point on I no longer avoided dying patients. Yes, I recognized that there would be painful moments, but somehow I would figure out a way to deal with them. I mused that perhaps I should be the doctor who appeared to be compassionate and mature enough to handle death. It really was that conscious of a career decision. As I think back on it, I shudder at the calculated coldness of this conclusion which was almost Machiavellian.

As far as I could see it was a win/win situation. Occasionally patients were going to die. In general, doctors had neither the time nor the inclination to immerse themselves in the dying process. Still, patients needed support. I would be admired by other doctors, nurses, and families if I were the one physician who could help them in their time of need. This, I decided, would be my role, and I got to be very good at it.

CHAPTER THREE

David

Soon after Alex died I began treating another child with cystic fibrosis. David was somewhat older, around sixteen. Throughout most of his early childhood his disease had been fairly well controlled, requiring very few admissions to the hospital. But the previous two years were sharply different. David was stricken with severe pneumonia each winter season, which left his lungs in a terribly weakened and vulnerable state. Each time it took David longer to recover, so he spent more time in the hospital. Unlike today, where people with this disease live well into their adulthood, we knew that David was reaching the extreme of his life expectancy. And we knew that with each bout of pneumonia he came closer to the end.

My earlier experience with Alex had prepared me for the eventuality of David's death. Or had it? I told myself early on in

David's care that I was not going to let myself, or him, get into the precarious situation that permission to die would be required from family members. As his physician it was my job to treat his pneumonia and lung deterioration as quickly and efficiently as possible. And as I learned from Alex, I equally had an obligation to prepare David and his family for the rapidly approaching certainty of his death. There was no doubt about what this meant: I would be in the very awkward position of assuring David and his family that while we were doing all we could to improve his condition, they were paradoxically in the excruciating position of having to prepare themselves for his impending death. Once again, it was the patient himself who helped me face this painfully unavoidable task.

David was a bright kid. He stood about 5 feet 7 inches, and was skinny as a rail (as all CF kids were in those days). He had sandy brown hair and a handsome face. He was very successful and popular at his high school. Coupled with the fact that he had two older siblings, his room was almost always filled with well-wishers. I remember enjoying the banter between David and his friends and sisters, thinking how wonderful it was for his spirits to be surrounded by such love and joy. Undoubtedly, it was precisely the potency of this love that prepared him to accept the ending of his life so courageously.

Upon reflection, it wasn't even David's courage, which was admirable enough; rather, it was his possession of a certain "knowledge" about his life, and its impending end. It would not be the last time that I was convinced that chronically ill kids know when their earthly sojourn is drawing to a close. It is as if they become the teachers, walking us, their students, through a process most people rarely witness. Not only are they the teachers, they also the healers.

They do in fact take over when our job as medical practitioners has exhausted its limitations.

And so it was with David's admission to the hospital. I was immediately aware that he knew it was to be his last. When he didn't respond to the antibiotics and breathing treatments after 48 hours in the hospital, he knew already that he wasn't ever going to respond. Unlike with Alex, I don't remember actually talking with David about it. It was just sort of understood between us. Physicians in general, and I am no exception, hate to deliver bad news. David's bad news did not require delivering. He could tell immediately upon my entering his room that his treatment was not going the way I would have liked. Whether he saw it on my face or in my mannerisms I will never know, but he knew. He seemed to know everything. Perhaps his inner self knew before even before checking into the hospital.

"How are your parents doing?" I remember asking him one day on rounds, not sure of how much understanding they had about this terminal stage of his disease.

"They know." He stated this quietly, almost in a whisper.

"They know?" I asked, a bit mystified by his response.

He looked up at me with a combination of resignation and sadness. "They know it's almost over," he continued. "They are not happy about it, but they know." The understatement of the century, I thought to myself. Apparently he had a similar thought, because he then smiled. In fact, he very nearly chuckled. This caught me completely off guard. I wondered if the family had openly discussed the subject of David's dying, or if they were possessed of the same sort of nonverbal "knowledge" that he was. I wanted desperately to ask him, just for my own edification, but it seemed like prying into their private moments. Asking him to recount their conversation felt like being a voyeur at their death bed lamentations, so I restrained myself. Still, I was curious. I could have learned so much, and later taught so much if I had known.

Eventually I did talk with the family. I remember David's father as a tall, robust, rather imposing gentleman, the kind that rarely displayed emotion. I suspected that he was a strict father, in a loving and nurturing way, but serious nonetheless. He worked for NASA, on the east coast of Florida, and seemed to possess the analytical characteristics of an engineer. Having been raised by an engineer myself, I effortlessly recognized these qualities.

David's mother was archetypal in her nurturing, maternal qualities, and I remember being drawn to her. She seemed the type that knew life had much to dish out, and it was a mother's job to keep the family always prepared for any eventuality. She exuded a conviction that although David's condition was tragic they would somehow get through it; they would become even stronger. She never actually said these things to me, yet I felt this from her, as I am sure David and his sisters also did. Still, no matter how strong, there is nothing that completely prepares someone for the moment of a loved one's death, for the extraordinary sense of finality of their loss. As David's departure approached, the entire family and a few close friends held vigil at his bedside. I happened to be on call that evening, but unlike many families sitting death-watch they didn't need me. They seemed fortified, prepared.

On the day David died he had been unconscious for many hours. Once his parents were certain that he could no longer respond to treatment—not even one last time—they requested he be designated a "DNR" (Do Not Resuscitate). They independently arrived at this decision without consulting the medical staff. Luckily, we agreed. (It would have been terribly unpleasant if we had not.)

Despite the bright, sunny day, David's room was cloaked in darkness by virtue of the closed blinds over his relatively small hospital room window. The room lights had been turned off, so the room was lighted only by the small amount of sunlight that flickered between the blinds. When I entered the room, I had to wait while my eyes adjusted to the dim lighting. The first silhouette I recognized was that of David's mom, who sat at his bedside holding his limp hand in hers. David's father stood at his son's bedside shifting his gaze from David to the three or four teenagers gathered at the foot of his bed. David himself reflected an aura of otherworldliness. He was even thinner than he had been when he was admitted, and his skin was almost snow white. He was in the characteristic "tripod" position of respiratory failure, and he would have been completely still were it not for the bobbing of his head and trunk with each respiratory movement, which had become rapid and shallow.

It is a somewhat merciful fact in respiratory failure that as the carbon dioxide in the bloodstream rises the brain essentially goes to sleep. I have often shared this fact to reassure parents who have made the decision to let their child die naturally without first placing them on a ventilator. Although the child appears to be working hard to breathe, in actuality they are aware of very little after the CO_2 reaches a certain level.

David's parents leaned into this knowledge for solace when the final moments finally approached. They reminded themselves of this phenomenon as David appeared to be working harder and harder and struggling more and more. They would later admit that despite their understanding of his disease at end stage, they were unprepared for how long or how hard David would struggle before he finally reached the end.

I happened to be in the room to witness David's last breath. The family had not asked me to be there; I just felt I should be. Moreover, I wanted to be there. After the pain of Alex's death and the horror of his mother, I had great admiration for the preparedness and strength of David's family. I wanted to see that. I wanted to experience it. I wanted to learn from it. There might be some pearl of knowledge their bravery and unselfishness would give me that would help me better serve dying patients and their families.

Indeed, they stayed strong right up until the end, which caught us all by surprise. I guess that we thought David's breathing would become shallower and shallower until it was difficult to determine if he was in fact breathing at all. But it actually happened much more abruptly than that. David's breaths were still quite deep. His head and shoulders continued to bob with each respiratory excursion. There was increasing time between each breath, which had the effect of making each breath appear deeper. Then, all of a sudden, as if someone flicked a switch, he stopped. His head bobbed up as he inspired, then slumped down with exhalation, never to rise again. Everyone in the room had become familiar with the rhythm of his pronounced respiratory effort, so when the next breath did not occur with the customary beat, all present at David's death watch suddenly hushed their murmuring and looked up. David's father, as prepared as he thought he was for this moment, was not.

"Oh my God, he stopped breathing," he stated in almost emotionless tones. "David, are you there?" He gently shook David's shoulder as he spoke to him, knowing full well the response to his question.

"I didn't think it would be like this!" David's dad exclaimed as he looked in my direction. I remember instantly feeling that I had somehow wronged him, and that the carefully orchestrated death scene had somehow gone awry. He didn't feel that way though. He just wasn't ready to accept that the son he had loved and raised for a decade-and-a-half was now gone. David's father cried first, the longest and loudest. All the strength in the world could not have prepared him for this final moment of letting go.

The family hugged me and thanked me as families often do in these circumstances. Yet in my heart I knew that I had done very little. Still, I accepted their thanks, wanting in turn to thank them for including me in their family at its most poignant moment. David had taught me much about death as being simply another phase of life. Moreover, he taught me about accepting one's destiny, and doing so with grace and trust. Death, I knew, would be unavoidable as I went through my training, and indeed throughout life. How I dealt with it would be the real issue.

CHAPTER FOUR

The Delivery Room

Soon after David's death I was required to rotate through the NICU again. Despite my earlier experiences with Felix Gomez, my first rotation through the unit had been a smashing success. For some reason it came very naturally to me. Besides, I loved it. Lives were saved daily. Whether it was rescuing a dying premature baby in the delivery room or placing a life-saving chest tube in a baby who had collapsed a lung while on a ventilator, drama and excitement were everywhere. The power was infectious. I was one of these who relished the drama and never missed an opportunity to be in the middle of it.

I particularly loved the delivery room. As pediatric residents in the NICU rotation, we would be called into the delivery room if any problems with the newborn were anticipated. This included situations such as extreme prematurity, respiratory difficulties, aspiration of meconium (fetal stool) and many other problems, including if the ob/gyn felt more comfortable with residents being in the room. For all C-sections we were asked to be present at the time of delivery. Babies born by not having gone through the mechanical chest compression that occurs when passing through the birth canal often require some respiratory stimulation and suctioning before they begin to breathe effectively on their own.

It was in the delivery room that I first learned to intubate babies, knowledge I would take with me when I later needed to place older kids on the ventilator. I will never forget the first time I actually performed this procedure successfully. A full-term baby was being born, which ordinarily would not require us to be in attendance. In this case, however, when the ob/gyn ruptured the mother's membranes (broke her water), he noted the presence of greenish meconium in the amniotic fluid. This was a warning sign that the baby had had a bowel movement while in the uterus, and there was a good chance some of this material could be aspirated into the lungs. It was our practice in those days to place a tube in the baby's trachea, a practice known as intubation, and suck the material from the windpipe and lungs.

Since I was still fairly early in my training, I followed the respiratory therapist into the delivery room fully expecting her to intubate while I assisted her in cleaning out the airway. We arrived in the delivery room just as the baby was being born. We quickly assembled our equipment in the warmer where we would receive the baby, checked the light on the laryngoscope blade, and made sure all suction equipment was operative. As the nurse wrapped the baby in towels and brought him to us, the RT very calmly looked at me and said, "OK, you're ready."

"Excuse me," I replied, incredulously.

"You're ready...you intubate this one," she stated authoritatively.

Immediately I was petrified. Part of me wanted desperately to learn this quintessentially lifesaving procedure, but other parts of me were terrified that I would be unsuccessful, or worse, cause harm. Clearly, I had no choice. The baby was on its way to the warmer, and the RT stepped back from the table, handing me the laryngoscope.

There was no time to think, no opportunity for negotiation. So I went for it. I dried the baby, who was crying and pink, thank goodness. I stabilized the baby's head with my right hand, pushing open his mouth with my forefinger. Thank goodness he doesn't have teeth, I thought to myself. I grasped the laryngoscope with my left hand and guided the blade along the baby's tongue. I gently lifted the tongue upward as I had been instructed, as the epiglottis popped off the blade in front of me. I knew I was in the right spot when I saw this, and expected to see the vocal cords fall into view. But where were they? I could see nothing but pink, amorphous tissue. And this crying angry baby was not appreciating this less than gentle welcome into his new world.

"I don't see the cords!" I said excitedly to my teacher-turned-assistant.

"Don't worry, the baby's fine. Just take your time." I could sense by the tone of her voice that she was smiling, but she remained just outside my peripheral vision, waiting patiently for me to succeed, or not.

When I was just about to give up, I saw what appeared to be a fold in what was otherwise a juicy, pink mess. That must be it, I thought to myself.

"Hand me the tube, please." I tried to sound confident to my mentor.

"Here it is. The stylet is in, and the tip is curved a little." Thank God she had taken time to do this for me, because this small maneuver makes it much easier for the tube to proceed along its desired path.

When I thought I was in the right place, I pushed the tube gently forward and miraculously, joyously, the baby stopped crying, signaling that the tube had indeed passed between the baby's vocal cords.

The RT then methodically ran the suction catheter down the tube and obtained clear fluid, which indicated that no meconium had passed below the cords. She passed the catheter down one more time for good luck, and we squirted some saline down the tube, suctioned once again, bagged with oxygen for a short time, then pulled the tube. I could have sworn that this newborn baby actually gave me a dirty look once the procedure was completed. What an indignity we had performed on this poor, unsuspecting child, even though it could have been lifesaving if the situation had been different. More importantly, what a triumphant moment I had.

We handed the baby to his grateful mother and proceeded back to the NICU. There have been very few moments in my life when I felt prouder than when I stepped back into that unit. I felt as if I had been accepted into an exclusive club whose members had mastered the intubation of babies! I now could, if called upon, truly save a life. After witnessing so much death so early in my training (or at least that's how it felt to me), I think for a moment I imagined that perhaps those days were behind me. No more kids had to die now that I knew how to intubate! Of course I didn't rationally believe this, but this feeling underscored the degree of power I felt in that moment. Further, my RT assistant seemed almost as proud as I was and couldn't wait to brag about me to my attending, Dr. A. When she told him how on the first attempt I completed my first intubation on a wide-awake, screaming, full-term, chubby, healthy newborn, he beamed. He placed his arm around me, told me how proud he was, and then warned me not to become complacent, or worse, cocky. The skill I had acquired was known by a select few, and was therefore to be respected.

As the days wore on, I had many opportunities to practice my new craft and never missed an opportunity to run to the delivery room to help respiratory therapy stabilize a newborn. In fact, I gained quite the reputation for being skilled in this department. Although I attempted to maintain a humble exterior, on the inside I was bursting with pride and new confidence, which could not have come at a better time. I had had my fill of dying patients and, although I felt more and more confident about being able to deal with such challenges, it was much more rewarding to save lives. After all, wasn't that the reason I went into medicine in the first place? Now, brandishing more skills and more experience, I was ready to be turned loose to save babies whenever I could.

It was later on in that same rotation that I was on call for the NICU and any emergencies that might occur with newborns any-where in the hospital, including, of course, the delivery room. It was about 3A.M. and I was lying in my call-room bed in that half sleep/ half waking state to which I had become accustomed. Through the wall of my cubicle I heard a voice pager go off which belonged to the ob/gyn resident on call for deliveries that night.

I could make out the voice on the pager stating, "DR stat for prolapse!" Within seconds I heard the resident running down the corridor to the delivery room. Almost immediately my pager sounded and then the same voice announced, "Peds to the DR, STAT!" It must be the same patient, I remember thinking. I knew enough to realize that whatever the mechanism, the umbilical cord had protruded from the uterus, causing blood flow to the fetus to be compromised. If the baby was not delivered in minutes there was high risk of death or at the very least severe brain damage from lack of blood flow. The ob/gyn resident was paged to get the baby out as quickly as possible; I was paged to save the baby, if possible.

When I arrived at the delivery room there was a sense of controlled panic pervading the atmosphere. The mother was already on the delivery/operating table, the ob/gyn residents were scrubbed and gowned. Anesthesia was administered to put the mother to sleep. Nurses were scurrying around preparing everything necessary to save this mother and her baby. I looked over to the infant warmer where the baby would be placed after the C-section. Nothing was prepared, and no one was in sight. Hasn't anyone thought about the baby? Where is my nurse? Where is my respiratory therapist? But before I could actually verbalize these questions, in what seemed like seconds the newborn infant was being pulled from this mother's now sliced-open uterus. I couldn't see much at first. As they held up the baby, I saw it was a boy, and that he was blue and making no effort whatsoever to breathe. The cord was cut. He was wiped off, wrapped in surgical towels heavily stained with blood, and placed in the warmer. The nurses were occupied with the mother. Respiratory therapy was tied up with another problem newborn.

Essentially, I was alone with what was basically a dead newborn. I looked under the warmer where the resuscitation supplies were kept, and saw a laryngoscope and endotracheal tube. Alongside was a mask and bag already hooked to oxygen. I grabbed the laryngoscope and the tube, barely taking time to dry off the baby. I proceeded to slip the endotracheal tube into this limp, blue baby. It took less than ten seconds to hook him up to the ambu bag with oxygen. I was already bagging the baby with O_2 when the respiratory therapist showed up. One of the nurses had left the mother and came over to beside the infant warmer with me. I asked one of them to bag so I could listen to the child's chest. There was good air exchange in both lungs which meant that the tube was in good position. I listened to the heart, but there were no heart sounds. I asked the nurse to stop bagging. I listened again, but still there were no sounds.

"We need to get a line," I said calmly to the nurse. "I'll bag; you get me an umbilical line catheter." I knew the fastest way to achieve IV access was through a large bore tube in the baby's umbilical vein, a technique I had learned only weeks before. Luckily the line went in easily and I began asking for drugs, epinephrine and sodium bicarbonate mainly. There was debate at the time about how much epinephrine should be used in a resuscitation effort such as this, even if there was a place for sodium bicarbonate in resuscitating a child whose respiratory status was questionable. I planned on using everything at my disposal. What harm could I cause, I thought to myself. This child was already dead and was most likely going to remain that way.

By now the attention in the room had begun to shift from the mother, who was clearly going to survive, to the baby, who did not yet have a heart rate and whose chances were questionable at best. A somber air began to fill the room as we worked. I heard murmuring amongst the ob/gyn residents as they closed the mother's belly. The mother was still asleep from the anesthesia. The feelings I was catching from the other side of the room were not hopeful ones. The pressure was mounting.

I was able to establish the umbilical line fairly easily. I flushed it with saline, then drew back on the syringe and obtained good blood return. It was time for the meds. We gave the first round of epinephrine and sodium bicarbonate…nothing. Second round… still nothing. I checked the ET tube for positioning… it was in good position. I listened for a heartbeat and felt for pulses…nothing.

The nurses gave each other knowing glances, which I tried to ignore. I knew what they were thinking. As each minute passed, the chances of survival decreased. Worse than that, the chances of irreversible brain damage increased. But I couldn't let this baby go. Up until a few minutes earlier, this mother thought she would be giving birth to a normal, full-term newborn, and then disaster struck. Besides, I had the tools to save this child. There existed no reason why I couldn't. Unless, I thought to myself, the blood supply to the fetus had been compromised for longer than we knew; unless the child was brain damaged even before we began the resuscitation. But I couldn't think about that now. I couldn't let myself get swept up in the negative feelings that had begun to overtake the room.

"Get me a 23 gauge, 3½" needle," I quietly asked the nurse standing next to me.

"What are you going to do?" she asked, somewhat concerned.

"I'm going to give intracardiac meds." I was curt and emotionless. "Please just get me the needle and a sterile syringe."

"John, I don't think…."

"Please get it for me, ok?" I'm sure she could hear the frustration in my voice. These nurses had great judgment. They knew the line between meaningful resuscitation and useless flogging of an already dead patient. The latter they considered cruel, and had seen enough of it in the name of physician education in their time. I was coming dangerously close to "cruel" in their minds.

I had seen intracardiac injection done only once. It was under slightly different circumstances, but the patient in that case was clearly dead. The attending suspected that the child may have died of a digitalis overdose. In order to prove it, he thought it best to obtain a sample of blood from within the heart itself. More than that, he could use the opportunity to demonstrate the procedure. For me, it was the chance to add another procedure to my cache. I tried not to pause long enough to consider the reality that there was a dead child at the other end of the needle.

So here was my chance to see one, do one, and teach one, as the saying goes. I had seen one, so now it was my turn to do one. The nurses looked at each other. I asked for Betadine and scrubbed the area at the base of the sternum. With my gloved fingers I felt for the notch between the sternum and the left side of the rib cage. I slowly advanced the needle upward and slightly toward the child's left shoulder, withdrawing on the syringe to create suction. I would know I was in the heart when I saw blood return in the syringe. Very soon I did, so I replaced the blood-filled syringe with one filled with epinephrine. I pushed down on the plunger of the syringe, injecting pure epinephrine directly into what I hoped to be the left ventricle. I pulled the syringe and needle out while the nurse continued to bag the child with oxygen. I asked her to stop while I listened to the chest. Once again, there were good breath sounds but no heartbeat. I asked for another syringe with epinephrine.

"John, are you sure you want…"

I cut her short. "Please just get me more epinephrine. I think we may get it this time." I truly did think this. I really wanted it. In such moments it is difficult to determine which emotion is most at play.

I did give the second epinephrine dose, and miraculously we got the child's heart beating again. It was a triumphant moment in the delivery room when the monitor began showing a normal EKG pattern. I just knew I could get that baby's heart beating again. It was only a matter of how much I wanted to do to make it happen, and how long I was willing to wait.

I felt like an absolute hero that night as I wheeled the baby into the NICU from the delivery room, pink, perfusing and with a good strong heartbeat. There may even have been applause from the NICU staff as we brought them the baby. Even if there hadn't been actual cheering, in my mind I felt like a general returning home after a glowing victory. In this case, the victory was over my resilient foe: death.

I went to speak to the baby's mother after she awakened and was returned to her room. She was puffy and visibly in pain, but her face bore the expression of relief and joy. "Thank you," was all she could muster before she burst into tears. I placed my arm on her shoulder and said nothing. I was Gary Cooper, John Wayne, and Spiderman all rolled into one. I had saved her baby boy and given him back to her. I couldn't have been prouder.

I walked back through the gyn ward, my feet barely touching the ground. The sunrise of a new day was beginning to filter through the windows of the nurses' station. The others would be arriving soon for morning rounds. My "save" of the night before would certainly be a hot topic of conversation. I couldn't wait. I felt as if I had surely arrived in the big time and was anxious to share my moment.

I turned the corner into the NICU and glanced to my left where the baby boy I had just saved was safely tucked into an iso-lette. He looked pink and comfortable. Suddenly, something caught my eye: his right foot was slightly twitching, and then the twitches became more pronounced. It was the beginning of his first seizure, which continued for hours that first day. It was followed by many more seizures that were increasingly difficult to treat, the kind one sees in an infant who has sustained brain injury. In this case irre-versible brain injury sustained when the brain has been deprived of oxygen and nutrients for too long—the kind of brain injury the nurses in the delivery room were worried about.

CHAPTER FIVE

Jared

It took me a long time to recover from that "save." And in some ways I haven't gotten over it yet. Should I have gone as far as I did? Is survival more important than anything? At what point during a resuscitation effort is it ethical to consider quality of life versus existence of life? In the heat of the moment, when our training kicks in to save life at any cost, when do we stop? There are no rules to answer these questions. There never can be. Legislators and judges will try to clarify such issues, but they will never succeed. There is no way all the contingencies can be covered. Every case, every scenario, every human is different, and the way they die is uniquely each one's own.

I have never found out how the baby boy from the delivery room did. If he survived today he would be nearly 25 years old, a young man with a career and possibly a family. Or, perhaps he was

profoundly mentally delayed as a result of my "save" and has spent
years in an institution or with assistance at home, with parents who
love him dearly and are now growing older and having medical
problems themselves. Or, was he even more profoundly affected,
bedridden and unable to feed himself? If he was this affected, he
probably isn't alive, having succumbed to pneumonia or some
other opportunistic infection or malady. I have no way of knowing
his outcome, and I never took the time to find out. In many ways,
I have never wanted to find out. I did my job in the delivery room
that day so many years ago. That is my only solace. I pray my young
patient has found peace somewhere.

Armed with this new knowledge—or confusion—of how to
handle dying children, I returned to the general pediatric ward
where, when on call, I covered the pediatric ICU. This was in the
days before the H. flu vaccine, and H. flu disease was commonplace
on our general peds service. H. flu is a bacterium. The full name is
Haemophilus influenzae, and it was a major cause of invasive disease in children up until the late eighties when the vaccine against
the bacteria became widespread. Perhaps the most devastating of
diseases caused by this bacterium was meningitis. Meningitis simply means inflammation of the coverings of the brain and spinal
cord, and can be due to any number of causes, including viruses,
fungi and bacteria. H. flu was simply one bacterium that could
cause meningitis, but it was known for its particularly aggressive
behavior, high morbidity and mortality. Barely a week passed that
we didn't have a child with H. flu meningitis. Most of these kids
were extremely sick. Many of them never went home.

Two-year-old Jared was infected by an incredibly virulent
bacterium that, if it didn't kill him, would leave him severely

handicapped for the rest of his life. His parents were young and dynamic, occupying important positions in the socio-economic strata of central Florida at the time. They were the kind of people who seemingly had it all. They were successful, financially comfortable, good-looking, and obviously in love with each other. They were the embodiment of the upper middle class American dream.

I no longer remember the details of how Jared became sick, but I can speculate because so often the pattern was the same. It no doubt began with a fever and fussiness, sometimes enough to warrant a visit to the pediatrician. Often something relatively inconsequential, like an ear or throat infection, was diagnosed, and equally often the patient was started on some sort of an antibiotic, like ampicillin. H. flu in that era was largely resistant to ampicillin, so if the patient was infected with that particular organism, it would continue to flourish despite the antibiotics. This was undoubtedly the case with Jared. Soon the irritability is replaced by sleepiness and the somnolence worsens until the child is unarousable. If medical attention was sought at this point, it was often too late. Damage to the central nervous system had already been done, and most of the time this damage was irreversible.

People who have seen the post-mortem examinations (autopsies) of patients who died of H. flu meningitis describe very similar findings. The brain and spinal column are coated with a thick, purulent rind, not unlike the skin of an orange, and the brain itself is infiltrated with areas of inflammation following the blood vessels meant to supply blood and nutrients to the fragile, but metabolically demanding nervous system.

When patients as sick as Jared arrived at the emergency department, they were comatose and barely breathing. They required intubation and ventilation, and if the infection was severe enough, medicine was given to maintain blood pressure and blood flow to vital organ systems. A spinal tap was performed, purulent spinal fluid was noted, and the lab verified that the gram stain revealed clumps of white blood cells intermingled with many gram negative rods, the bacteria itself. Antibiotics were administered immediately following the spinal tap, causing the patient to show some improvement, since the bacteria almost always die after antibiotics are started. Survival might have been achieved, but a return to previous full function was far more dubious and uncertain.

I met Jared when he was at this stage, although the acute infection had abated and he was no longer getting any worse. However, the damage had been done, and it was severe. He had been extubated so was able to breathe, and could maintain his blood pressure and other vital functions on his own. Nevertheless, he was largely unresponsive. He could not feed himself, nor even be fed by mouth. A nasogastric tube and IV fluids were required to maintain basic nutrition and hydration. By the time Jared completed his mandatory ten days of IV antibiotics, he was no longer infected, but he was essentially a vegetable.

I myself did not have direct responsibility for Jared, but I heard about him each day on rounds and thanked God that I didn't have to deal with his predicament and with his family. In the aftermath of my experiences the past few months, I would not have been able to deal with how difficult this was going to be for his family. Jared was not going to die, that seemed certain, yet it did not appear likely that his neurological condition would improve very much. Back then we were taught—and conveyed to our patients and their families—that the number of neurons a person possesses at birth is finite and decreases throughout life. Once these neurons are destroyed by any kind of hypoxic/ischemic event, they never regenerate. Thus, any brain damage that occurred from this kind of event was static; it would never improve. Today we feel differently about brain injury and realize that although neurons and brain tissue may not regenerate, there are tremendous possibilities for retraining the brain and re-mapping lost neuronal pathways.

As far as we could determine from the information we had at the time, Jared's chances for survival were nil. His parents were fully aware of this, even though none of his caregivers had the courage to come right out and state this to them unequivocally. But it was not like any major decisions needed to be made since Jared did not require a ventilator, or extreme measures to keep him alive. Although it was true that he would never be able to communicate effectively with his parents or with the rest of the world, with adequate fluid, nutrition, and hydration Jared could be kept alive indefinitely.

There were other problems, however, that offered challenges in Jared's management. He had an extremely difficult time dealing with his own secretions, or any material in his mouth and throat. He had lost the ability to swallow and effectively protect his airway and windpipe. As a result, the PICU nurses had to stand almost constant vigil suctioning out Jared's mouth and nose, because without this suction he would have obstructed his airway, been unable to breathe, and would have died. Even his mother, who had no prior medical experience or training, became quite adept at suctioning Jared's nose and throat.

As is the case with these kinds of patients—those who are no longer acutely ill but also have no hope for meaningful survival—

the medical staff, particularly in a teaching setting, begins to lose interest. If there are no new interesting problems, the patient is barely discussed on rounds. I had experienced this just before Alex died and resented the practice. Now, however, I was perfectly happy to breeze past Jared's bed without spending much time talking about him. After all, his case was exceedingly depressing and there was really nothing we could do for him. He was a vegetable, would always be so, so the quicker we could get him transferred home or to some other institution the better.

The nursing staff had a different view of Jared's case. They had taken time to get to know the family and to understand where they were coming from. Even when the intellectual details of Jared's illness were no longer interesting to the physicians, the nurses still had to take the time to care for all of his bodily needs, twenty-four hours a day. And since his mother or father sat vigil at his bedside every minute of the day, the nursing staff got to know the family quite well and hence to understand their predicament and their intense, almost indescribable sadness.

As far as Jared's parents were concerned, his life had ended. He was no longer the little boy they had known before he got sick, and from all that they were told by the medical staff, he never would be. A boy who had only weeks before been running and playing in their yard was now inanimate, and required constant suctioning just to keep from drowning in his own secretions and choking to death. This was not the way they wanted the child they loved to live his life; they wanted his suffering to be over. They shared their feelings openly with the nursing staff, who in turn conveyed them to the medical staff. But to no avail. There was simply nothing that could be done. Jared was in a static state where very little was done to keep him alive. This was not a case where an endotracheal tube could be removed, medicines discontinued, or even a ventilator stopped. There was seemingly no easy, medically justifiable way that Jared's death could be hastened any quicker than nature intended.

In reality, though, there were two ways that Jared's life could end (barring anything unforeseen that would just stop his heart): either he would become obstructed from the thick secretions unable to be cleared from his throat and suffocate; or, he would starve. The latter seemed cruel because it required active measures and was therefore unthinkable. The former was simply nature taking its course. Jared's parents had decided, then, that essentially Jared's life was over. They wanted no more heroic measures taken to prolong it. If there had been a way to precipitate his demise, they were of a state of mind that would have considered it. They knew that eventually his airway would become obstructed by his own secretions and because of his inability to protect it, and that would be the end.

One of the reasons that doctors avoid the kind of situation Jared and his family found themselves in is completely understandable: it is unbearably painful to watch a family deal with such an untenable situation day in and day out. There were no easy solutions to Jared's predicament and every physician on the team knew that he had no chance for meaningful life. And since there was no solution, the only option was avoidance. By the end, barely a word was spoken about Jared on rounds. No formal directive was ever given, but by ignoring Jared and his family more obviously each day, the family understood that they were being left to deal with this "problem" in the best way they saw fit. Essentially, the medical team was wordlessly saying, "He's now your problem."

I remember the day Jared died as very anticlimactic. Even though I was on the PICU service that month, I didn't hear about his death until much later in the day, long after his heart had stopped. Certainly, no one was surprised by Jared's death. In fact, most people seemed relieved, and even a bit happy that the parents' ordeal was finally over.

It wasn't until weeks later that I learned of the circumstances of Jared's last day. His parents knew he was not going to survive, and they could no longer bear watching him suffer. Although they wanted no active measures taken to artificially prolong his life, they knew they did not have sympathetic listeners on the medical staff. After all, wasn't it the doctors' job to preserve life at all cost? There was no way that Jared's parents could convince the doctors to help them make Jared's death easier and more merciful. It would have to be the nursing staff, the true "souls" of the hospital.

The nurse who was assigned to Jared when he died had taken care of him for many days. She had become very comfortable with him, his parents, and the tremendous love that existed in their family. She, too, knew that Jared's life was over, despite what his medical report suggested. It wasn't that his parents wanted any active measures taken; they simply wanted his suctioning to be less aggressive, for his nurse to respond less quickly when alarms sounded, and when his heart stopped they didn't want him "coded." (This was one directive that the medical staff had no difficulty complying with.)

I am told that when Jared died his mother and father were at his side. So was this one angel of a nurse who did everything she could to make him comfortable, but nothing excessive that would prolong his life. His parents watched him die and knew he did so comfortably and without pain. His nurse became one of their dearest friends for loving Jared in such a profound way. In fact, she became one of the best nurses that institution had ever seen. And, several years later, she became my wife.

CHAPTER SIX

Michael

The word "gork" is an ugly term rarely heard outside the hospital setting. In fact, it is rarely heard outside of teaching hospitals filled with young residents, interns, medical students and fellows who are all striving to achieve their own understanding of the human drama. A gork is a patient—a human being—who has for whatever reason lost most of his or her higher mental functions. To be categorized this way means that an individual lacks basic communication skills, the ability to get around, and the ability to care for themselves. Sometimes patients in this condition are cared for in the family home, or if their disability is profound they must be cared for in an institutional setting.

In the medical culture a gork is considered a failure, much like a dying patient is a failure. Doctors are trained not only to preserve life, but to preserve quality of life, which typically means that when treating life-threatening illness or injury the brain must be preserved in order for medical success to be proclaimed. It is my opinion that "gork" is used as a physician's defense mechanism. The patient who has lost higher brain function is best dealt with by depersonalizing, dehumanizing him or her. To the medical team caring for such a patient, it is easier to apply this term rather than a name, or even a gender. One doesn't have feelings for an inanimate object. And when there are no feelings, there can be no pain.

Had Jared survived his meningitis, he most likely would have been severely disabled. His medical team might have referred to him in the third person—though not in the presence of his family—as a "gork." Perhaps his family grasped his fate, or maybe they simply knew he would never again be the child who loved life and laughed every day. Jared was fortunately saved this indignity.

When I met Michael, he could have been placed in the unofficial gork category. Although he recovered from meningitis, he was left severely damaged by the disease. I did not take care of him during his acute illness, but the stories circulated about him were well known. Michael was admitted from his pediatrician's office extremely sick. His spinal tap was positive for meningitis, but none of the usual infecting organisms grew from the initial culture. Because of the chemical and cellular pattern of the spinal fluid, the infectious disease consultants speculated that perhaps mycobacterium tuberculi, the bacteria that causes tuberculosis, might be the causative organism. Anti-tuberculosis meds were started, but hopes were not high for a significant recovery from his infection.

Once it appeared that the infection was under control and Michael was getting no worse, it was also clear that he had been irreversibly damaged by the disease. The treatment for TB meningitis is prolonged, so there remained time to fully assess Michael's status, and to promote his neurological recovery. If there was to be any meaningful recovery, his rehabilitation was going to have to be intensive and long term. Throughout his many weeks of antibiotics, Michael never fully recovered and remained severely disabled.

Michael was two years old when he got sick, and as in so many similar cases, he was completely healthy before being ravaged by the disease. His family lived in a small town outside of Orlando that, during the population boom of the 80's, quickly became a bedroom community for the burgeoning metropolis of the new south. His father was a successful businessman and a pillar of the community, and his mother was a devoted mother to Michael and his older sister.

Michael's family had done everything right in raising him. (Even before he was born, his mother had been extremely conscientious about her health, assuring that her pregnancy was optimal.) They had hooked up with one of the more dynamic pediatrician groups in town and were dedicated to his well childcare. He received all of his shots, experienced only a couple of colds, and was growing well above the fiftieth percentile for both height and weight.

Michael had been walking for over a year and was into everything. His speech had progressed rapidly over the prior two months and he was quite adept at getting his point across to his adoring family. Like all two-year-olds, he was in love with life and his world. He was a joy to all who knew him and loved by many. By the time he was stricken with this tragic disease, the effects were felt by those in his small, close-knit community. It was not just a tragedy for the family, but for the entire town.

When Michael was discharged his family assumed they would take Michael back to their general pediatrician for follow-up. He still needed routine care, and a medical quarterback to coordinate his complex post-hospitalization care and rehabilitation. Sadly, it seemed that the pediatricians were uncomfortable caring for someone like Michael. His problems were too complex, and in one pediatrician's opinion, the parents' expectations were unrealistically high. At least that is what he told our residency program director when he requested that Michael become enrolled in the residents' pediatric clinic, which is how Michael became my clinic patient.

During Michael's prolonged hospitalization I was on call several days when he required attention. I don't remember the particular details of our interactions, nor do I remember trying to conduct myself in any particular way when caring for him. Something about my conduct appealed to Michael's parents, so they asked if I would be his clinic doctor. I accepted. (The reality was that I really didn't have much choice in the matter.) How difficult could it be, I thought to myself. The family hired round-the-clock nurses at home, and they had become quite savvy in his care. All I would have to do was see Michael for his scheduled appointments and be available to them if he got sick. I'm sure other residents joked with me about patients like Michael—they were easy, they would say. After all, how badly can you mess up a gork?

I was not prepared for the impact of seeing Michael in my clinic for the first time. He arrived with both of his parents and one of his nurses. His reason for the visit was that he was experiencing cold symptoms and running a bit of a fever. His parents were concerned that he might have an ear infection, or worse, pneumonia. If necessary, they wanted him on antibiotics before things got too out of control.

I approached the examining room door with little apprehension. Most likely I was thinking about a patient I was caring for on the ward, or how I could get myself into the good graces of the nurse I had been attracted to, or what kind of car I might buy when my rusted-out wreck finally died alongside the road. I was not thinking about Michael or his predicament. But when I opened the examining room door all thoughts instantly vanished from my mind.

Michael was more profoundly disabled than I had expected. His skin was pale and doughy. His arms were pulled up to his chest and were tightly flexed. His legs were bent at the knees and stiff, and his feet were toeing downward. He was much chubbier than he had been in the hospital, by virtue of the formula he was fed through the tube that protruded from the left side of his abdomen. His head was arched backward somewhat, and his eyes flickered involuntarily. His dark brown hair was neatly combed. His hygiene, in fact, was impeccable. He had a tracheotomy tube protruding from his neck, and the white ties that held it in place were clean and neatly tied. His breathing was shallow and slow, interrupted by an intermittent sigh or cough, the vibrations of which could be heard through the trach tube.

Michael could not eat on his own because his swallowing mechanism had been lost as a result of the infection. The trach was inserted because he was unable to deal with his own secretions, and it gave his caregivers access to clear his airway. He was fed through a gastrostomy tube which eliminated any ability to participate in the most fundamental of nurturing behaviors: feeding one's baby. He had no purposeful motions, only involuntary ones. He did not verbalize except for the gurgles resonating through his tracheotomy. He could not respond to voices, or light, and only occasionally did he respond to touch. It was unpredictable whether he would become calm or agitated by the touch of another human. He was, in the parlance of my fellow professionals, a complete gork. And now this gork was my patient.

I absolutely believe that Michael was sent to me for a reason. It is said that when the student is ready, the teacher appears. Michael was there to be my teacher. There was something else in the room that day, another element besides the devices designed to give Michael comfort and to keep him alive: Love. I became aware of this soon after getting over the initial shock of seeing him in his current condition. Once my gaze moved from Michael to his parents and his nurse, I realized that all three of them were smiling. These weren't the disingenuous, polite smiles that come from people who are somewhere they would rather not be. They were the genuine smiles that come from those who feel true joy, the kind of joy found in families who love each other so much that they relish every moment they are together.

But how could they feel this way? How could they appear so joyful, I thought to myself. Why weren't they angry? Why weren't they resentful? Why didn't they have a chip on their shoulders when dealing with medical caregivers, like so many others do in such situations?

It was months before I received answers to these questions. The final answers, in fact, didn't come to me until Michael's funeral. I had gotten to know Michael's family quite well during the time between his first clinic visit and his eventual death. As expected, he was frequently sick, so required my seeing him in the clinic almost weekly. Many of those visits resulted in hospital admissions. His last admission was for pneumonia, and I knew the minute I saw him that he wasn't going to survive that particular bout. The family had made him a DNR several weeks before, so I knew that without ventilatory support he was not going to survive this pneumonia.

The amazing thing about his family was that they seemed to know these things before I did. In fact, the day I was going to talk to them about Michael's inevitable demise they had already begun to make funeral arrangements, part of which was to designate honorary pallbearers. They asked if I would consider accepting such a role, and of course I did. I was deeply moved to have been asked, although I never felt that I was completely qualified for this honor.

It was during the eulogy given by Michael's father that I finally began to understand the peace that this family felt, even in the midst of their tragedy. It turned out that they had profound faith. They knew that God had a plan for them, and all they could do was to pray to accept this plan. They loved their little Michael when he was given to them, and wished they could have watched him grow into the fine young man they knew he would become. Sadly, that wasn't to be. But they did not love him any less because he had gotten sick and was so damaged. In some ways they loved him more. More importantly, they knew that he loved them. They never stopped talking to him and telling him that they loved him, right up until the very end of his earthly existence, and even beyond. Sure, they grieved over losing him, but his brief time with them had brought them great joy, and he had made them better people, for which they were grateful.

Michael changed me, too. In some ways, my relationship with him brought me more questions than answers. How could a human, with whom I was never able to have a conversation, who had never been able to smile at me, have such a profound impact on me? The love this family shared made me envious, and made me wonder if I would ever experience that kind of love in my life. I made this promise to myself the day of Michael's funeral: The term "gork" would be forever abolished from my vocabulary. And I learned one more thing: No child can ever be forsaken as long as he or she is loved.

As my residency drew to a close I felt as if I had received an unexpected and largely unwelcome education in dealing with death, while simultaneously attempting to learn treatments and patient management designed to avoid death. The latter, I thought, was the whole point of my medical training, while the former was an unwelcome necessity. Yet, if truth be told, few of my questions about death and dying patients had been effectively answered. I resisted the temptation to consider what it all meant to my life and to my own mortality, and to the mortality of those I loved. It was much easier to distance myself from the human reality of illness and death. A doctor cannot be a good doctor, I decided, if he thinks of himself as a potential patient, and therefore mortal. There was no escaping the reality of death, yet I needed to learn how to treat sick children so as to prevent it at all cost. Would I ever reach a true understanding of life and death to such a degree that I could effec- tively care for my patients? This remained the driving question behind my training and on into my practice. In fact, it would became the driving question of my life.

CHAPTER SEVEN

Emily

Emily was a three-year-old blonde tomboy, and the apple of her dad's eye. They lived in the country on a farm with lots of animals and lots of machinery. Emily's dad kept his supplies of insecticides, gasoline, oil, etc., behind the house in a shed well out of reach of children, and always locked... except this one day. The shed door was left open just enough for the very mobile Emily to find her way in. Emily's dad prescribed to the unsafe but popular practice of leaving gasoline and other petroleum products in coke bottles. The temptation of the open soda bottle on the floor of the shed was more than Emily could resist. She gulped down a mouthful of kerosene mixture from the coke bottle. She immediately gasped and coughed, allowing for the volatile fumes of the very noxious substance to flow freely into her lungs.

In our business this scenario is referred to as a "hydrocarbon aspiration," and is one of the truly dreaded pediatric intensive care conditions. Hydrocarbon-based substances are incredibly injurious to mucus linings with which they come in contact, particularly the lungs. The fumes from these substances are extremely volatile, and they easily drift into the tiny airways of the lungs. They are terribly noxious to these airways, damaging the cells that produce surfactant, a substance necessary to keep airways and alveoli open. With further tissue destruction, air leaks outside the lungs into the chest cavity, sometimes causing the lungs to collapse. In short, hydrocarbons devour lung tissue. This is indeed what was happening to Emily when I met her.

I was in my fellowship in pediatric critical care medicine at the University of Florida when I met Emily. It was our job as fellows to be at the resident's side when sick children were admitted to the ICU and to assist in their care. We were the liaison between the attending, who was ultimately responsible for all patient care during his/her watch, and the residents, who were very inexperienced and mainly interested in learning how to be good general pediatricians. Consequently, most of the actual bedside care, particularly with the very ill patients, fell to us, the fellows.

Emily was transferred from an outlying rural hospital where she had already been intubated and placed on a ventilator. Her blood gases were terrible and she was barely able to maintain enough oxygen in her blood stream for survival. She required very high ventilator pressures to keep her lungs minimally aerated and her chest X-ray already demonstrated some of the air was leaking, as is classically seen with this problem.

"You'll be able to fix her up, right Doc?" Emily's father pleaded even before she had been taken off the transport stretcher. He was a simple, down-to-earth man from the country, and he looked the part, from his John Deere hat to his stained and faded coveralls. His eyes, however, were soft and kind, betraying his attempts to appear gruff and confident.

"You know she only took a small amount of the stuff before she started gagging and coughing. I can't imagine there's much in there." His guilt was palpable. He looked down at his mud-caked work boots. "Who would have ever thought a little bit of that stuff could be so bad...."

I tried to reassure him, but I knew from the other hospital's report and now seeing Emily that we were in for a long haul. I used all my best lines: "We'll do the best we can" and "It's really too early to tell," which seemed to appease him. Yet I wondered if he caught the contradictory worry in my eyes that I certainly could see in his.

Emily went through hell, and consequently so did her father. He never left her bedside except during procedures or when we made rounds with the PICU team. He completely neglected his farm during the weeks that she was in the hospital, telling us it really didn't matter because if Emily, his pride and joy, didn't make it, nothing else would matter anyway.

Unfortunately, in hydrocarbon aspiration there is no known way to "heal" the lungs once they have been injured by the poisons. The trick to management is to try to keep the patient alive long enough to allow the lungs to heal on their own. The challenge is that this requires aggressive respiratory support which, in itself, can damage the lungs. So, the more we did to keep Emily going, the worse her lungs became, making her survival less likely. Naturally, when each day families see that their loved one is still alive, they build hope that they will ultimately survive. In Emily's case the opposite was true.

Predictably, Emily's death would occur in one of two ways: either she would have a cardiac arrest or complete circulatory shut down because her lungs could not provide enough oxygen to keep vital functions operational; or we would run out of things to do for her, and with no hope for recovery she would slowly deteriorate and we would begin to back off life support and let nature take its course. At this point, Emily had tubes and lines running from every orifice along with maximal respiratory support. (We even tried the high frequency jet ventilator and oscillator, both of which were experimental in 1985.)

Medicines were required to keep Emily's blood pressure up and she was on continuous sedation and pain medication to keep her comfortable. More horrifying was the way she looked. As her lungs became more damaged and leaked more air into the chest cavity, she required five chest tubes to evacuate it. Air began leaking out into the tissues under her skin, puffing her up like a balloon. She no longer appeared anything like the little girl her father had brought to the hospital days before. He had to know the end was near.

In my conversations with Emily's father, I tried to guide him to that realization. We had decided that to do anything more aggressive with Emily would be cruel. We were not all in agreement on this. Those who had worked with her the longest and experienced the sensation of plunging stiff tubes into her chest cavity to evacuate air felt that the time had come to withdraw support. I was in this group. Others felt we should keep trying because her lungs might turn around, or some other modality of treatment might become available to us if we could just keep her alive long enough. Interestingly, this group included those who were the least comfortable discussing death with either the team or with family members.

Ultimately, the decision rested with the father. It was up to me to convince him that all that could be done had been done, and that at this stage Emily should be made comfortable. More importantly, I was hoping to solicit his agreement that nothing more aggressive should be done for Emily, and that we should even begin to consider withdrawing life support.

At first, he was completely resistant to any suggestion that there was nothing more that we could do. "Doc, I know you guys can fix her...that's why we came to this place...they all spoke so highly of you here." He almost began to whine. We were his last hope. It was gut-wrenching, but it was useless. "Look, sir..." I had discovered that to get a parent to do what we thought was right they had to be led, all the while careful to let them feel as if they were responsible for any final decisions. "I know you love Emily very much. I know you want her to get better. But, just as it's our job to provide the best care for her, it is also our job to be honest with you. And the fact is there isn't anything left for us to do that could save Emily...." I let my voice trail off, leaving her dad to fill in the silence with the obvious.

"She's going to die, isn't she, Doc?" It was always better when they said the "d" word before I had to. I felt I had good rapport with this man—thank God I was right. "I'm afraid she is, sir." I put my hand on his shoulder and tried to give him a comforting smile. I couldn't stop there, unfortunately. I needed more out of him.

"There's something else we need to talk about," I said with my hand still on his shoulder. I glanced away from him in the general direction of Emily. "What's that, Doc?" He looked incredibly tired to me. He sensed that anything else I would say would be bad news.

"As we said a moment ago, it looks as if Emily is going to die, and probably soon. So now we have some decisions to make." "OK, Doc, whatever you say," he replied with a heaving sigh.

"Well, first we have to decide what we are going to do if…well, when her heart stops." I didn't want to lose momentum. We were in one of those rare moments where total trust exists between physician and family member. It will always be true that the best decisions and the most healing ones are born during those miraculous moments. It is in such moments—where insurance companies and attorneys will never be—that the true magic of medicine takes place. It has taken me years to understand this, so I doubt I was aware of the profoundness of the moment when I spoke with Emily's dad. I was simply trying to manipulate him to my way of thinking.

"What do you mean?" He was understandably puzzled. "I thought you already said that there was nothing more that could be done for her."

"I did say that." I had to be careful not to lose him now. "What I am referring to is the end…when her heart finally stops. The hospital has protocols and procedures for such things. When someone dies the staff is obliged to perform a full resuscitation on the patient. In other words, unless there are orders on the chart to do otherwise, she will be given medicines to keep her heart going and her chest will be thumped until she is completely gone. Do you understand?"

He gazed over toward his daughter, now a bloated, ghostly, faint reminder of the beautiful child who had been his reason to get out of bed each morning. I could almost visualize his thoughts:

images of a "code" like the ones he had seen on TV, crowds of anonymous medical people crowded around a dying person's bed giving them one last pummeling before death, just "doing their job" as the patient's life slowly ebbs away.

"I don't want you to do that to my Emily." His words were nearly catatonic. "Leave her be. Let her die in peace." There, that was what I needed. I had my "do not resuscitate" order, the first step. But I wasn't done yet. "I agree completely with you, sir, she should not have to suffer any more. But now we need to think about something else."

This time he looked up at me with much less benevolence, as if he was at the losing end of a negotiation. As the terms were being spelled out to him, he was reminded of the magnitude of his loss. This time his expression took on the character of a scowl. "What else?" His terseness bespoke his emotional fatigue.

"Well, it's just that I'm not sure that any of what we are doing is doing her any good anymore." I was on much shakier ground now. I think he sensed my insecurity.

"I know, Doctor." The new formality of his speech worried me. For a moment I thought he might go back on all the agreements we had just made. "I thought we just went through all that." "Yes, you're absolutely right, we have." I practically bowed before him. "But I am kind of referring to something else." I needed to continue and get my point across before he got cold feet. "All this we are doing prolongs her life, it's true. But eventually even this won't work. Her lungs are gone, her heart is barely functioning, and even if we saved her, her brain may never be what it once was. She is not the little girl you brought in here…." I was about to say, "and she never will be," when he grabbed my arm.

"You want to turn her off, don't you?" He was looking at Emily, not at me. "Unplug her from all these machines, huh?"

"No, sir, nothing quite that dramatic." Poor choice of words. He looked at me as if I was mocking him. I had to continue. "No. But I think we should begin to back off on some things. We will keep her comfortable. That will be our first priority." (I was angry at myself for not saying this earlier.) "But I'm afraid there really isn't any more point to all this, and I don't think you want to put her through any more than she must go through."

"I never wanted to have her go through all this shit. I didn't want her to drink the kerosene…and I certainly don't want her to die." His eyes filled with tears. "But I don't want her be tortured… no more…no more." He muttered as his voice got lost in the handkerchief he pulled from the pocket of his overalls.

I didn't want him to cry in front of me, but it was inevitable that he would once the reality of our conversation hit home. I put my arm on his shoulders and looked toward the nurses' station for some help. One of the more seasoned staff had been watching our conversation from a distance. She took Emily's dad by the arm saying something about a drink of water and motioned him out of the unit. As he passed me she smiled, nodding in acceptance. I had done a good job. She approved. I may not have been able to handle every illness and every problem that came up in the PICU, but one thing was for sure: I knew how to handle dying patients.

Emily died forty-eight hours later. We were able to slowly wean her off the ventilator without removing her completely. Emily was stable enough that her dad was able to hold her in his lap one last time. That was a tough scene to handle. We stopped making rounds on Emily. As with Alex years before, when there is nothing more to be said, when there is nothing more medically that can be done, the patient ceases to be an integral part of the medical work day. Moreover, we don't want to be reminded of yet another defeat at the hands of the Grim Reaper.

Still, it wouldn't have been right for me to ignore him. He had given me what I needed to complete my care of the patient. I owed him at least a touch or a kind word. And so I gave that to him. What I remember most clearly are the pictures that he brought in and placed around the bed: Emily smiling, playing with her dolls, being kissed by her puppy…being alive. The most startling image was Emily's dad smiling, the pain of the previous days gone, the peace and the love that filled him spilling out. I didn't understand it. In a way it frightened me. I prided myself in my handling of dying patients, yet I understood nothing about death. At that point in my development as a physician it was not so important that I understood death, as it was that I figure out a way to deal with it.

And deal with it I did.

CHAPTER EIGHT

Amy, Cindy, Joey

When my fellowship finally ended it was not clear where my career would take me. I thought I would go back to my residency program because I knew they needed help in the PICU. The program, however, was on shaky ground and the politics were intense, so I approached my former training ground with caution.

I was now a newlywed. Pam and I met during residency and went off to fellowship together where she worked as a nurse in the PICU. Our next location would require jobs for both of us. So, due to a combination of factors—not the least of which was our own pickiness and apprehension—the first two months after my training as a physician we were both unemployed. It was not a completely desperate period, although I admit I was somewhat of a basket case during this time. I was haunted by self-doubt and insecurity, qualities with the potential to make me almost impossible to live with.

Finally fate took a turn and a letter came from a large community hospital in Louisville, Kentucky. The general pediatricians there decided that they needed a newly trained pediatric ICU doctor to assist them with their sick children. Prior to this time, ICU trained physicians were in larger, tertiary care centers connected to medical schools and universities. (Treating the critically ill was tied in to teaching and research and therefore belonged at universities, the purists argued.) Community practitioners and community hospitals wanted to hang on to critically ill patients, primarily for financial reasons, so they recruited intensive care trained physicians to care for them in their facilities, thus obviating the need for transfer. I was to fulfill this role for them.

I was recruited, and heavily courted. Fresh out of training—not to mention naïve, fearless and cocky—I thought I could do anything and care for anyone. All that was required were the right tools, and I was given carte blanche to obtain them. So during my first months on staff we recruited and trained nurses, designed, and began construction on a state-of-the-art PICU.

To care for these patients effectively we needed personnel. It took considerable effort to convince the hospital administration that one pediatric intensivist alone could not take care of every aspect of every sick child. They somehow thought that this "super doctor" was a great economical choice. Unfortunately, I burst their bubble with my insistence that subspecialists were also needed. These included: pediatric cardiologists, pulmonologists, infectious disease specialists, surgeons, ENT specialists, neurologists, and emergency room physicians who would be available to come to our hospital to care for our patients just as they would for any sick child at the university children's hospital. In essence, we had to create a private, community-based version of a university teaching hospital but without the teaching! In 1985, this concept—especially in Louisville, Kentucky—was unheard of. (Today it is commonplace.)

For these subspecialists, whom we recruited enthusiastically, the attraction was that they would have a private practice, bill for their services, and still care for the type of patients they liked to see. The medical insurance revolution was in full force and managed care was on the horizon. Universities were financially strapped and hospitals were trying to be as diverse as possible so as to attract third-party payers. Families wanted the convenience of remaining in their own communities when their children were sick, rather than having to travel to distant university settings. And everybody was scrambling to get their piece of what was perceived as the shrinking health care dollar.

Why is all this relevant? Because as I began my career in private practice, I was given the opportunity to literally design a new unit. To do so I needed to be cognizant of every detail necessary for superior patient care. Moreover, I needed to become a good businessman. Caring for patients was beyond just good medicine: there were politics involved! The referring pediatricians needed to be happy; they needed to feel that their patients were well cared for. Parents needed to be satisfied in order to give positive feedback to their primary care physician. Nurses needed to feel they were learning, being challenged, and appreciated. The subspecialists needed to feel that their practices would prosper, and the insurance companies needed to feel that they were getting good value. The hospital administration needed to feel it was getting good public relations, and most of all, that it was making money. In the framework of all this, I had to develop a strategy for dealing with the inevitable consequence of tackling such a major undertaking as the PICU: dying children.

We had our fair share of tragedies. One poignant case involved two almost identical three-year-old girls. By a haunting coincidence, they both came down with a terrible infection within twenty-four hours of each other.

Meningococcemia is caused by the bacteria N. meningitides, and is one of the most dreaded and still deadly infections faced by pediatricians. Ironically, despite the name, it does not necessarily cause meningitis. In its most deadly form it causes sepsis, or an overwhelming infection of the bloodstream that eventually affects all the body's organ systems. One of the most terrifying aspects of this illness is its virulence. Children can be perfectly well in the morning, develop a rash and fever by noon, be in shock by mid-afternoon and, without proper immediate care, be dead by midnight. Sometimes it progresses even faster. The good news is that this infection is exquisitely sensitive to antibiotics, and if administered in a timely manner the chances for full recovery are good. Still, the mortality rate of a full-blown infection is high. While today we now have a vaccination against this infection, this was not the case in the late 1980's.

Amy and Cindy both had meningococcemia. Amy came through the emergency room and the staff suspected the infection the minute they saw her. She had a high fever all night and upon arrival in the ER she was pale with small reddish purple spots on her chest and extremities. What concerned her parents even more than her seemingly otherworldly appearance was her combative behavior, which was so unlike her usual sweet demeanor. What they didn't realize was that these were all signs of shock. It is this shock state that needs to be attacked aggressively if there is to be any hope of recovery. (To this day, septic shock remains one of the most deadly of acquired illnesses.)

The ER called me immediately upon her arrival and we admitted her directly to the PICU where IV lines were placed and fluids administered. Antibiotics were given along with medicines to stabilize her blood pressure. As we titrated fluids and managed her medicines, we sweated it out at the bedside. Often, once optimal care is delivered, it simply takes time to see what the response will be to treatment. In Amy's case, miraculously, the response was favorable, though not completely. Unfortunately, she lost function of her kidneys, so we had to transfer her to the children's hospital for dialysis. She survived, much to her parents' relief.

The second child, Cindy, was nowhere near as fortunate. She didn't make it. What made it even more tragic was that we had done exactly the same things for her as we had done for Amy. Medicine will never be an exact science. No matter how much we observe and learn, there remain powers beyond our own. We in medicine like to think that we are always in control, that we can solve every problem, fight every infection. The older and more experienced I become the more I realize this to be a monumental fallacy.

I remember Cindy's deathbed like it was yesterday. Her parents were young. She was the oldest child of two and clearly the apple of her father's eye. From the moment she was admitted he never left her bedside. And when it became clear that she probably wouldn't survive despite our heroic efforts, he broke down and sobbed.

"No, it can't be true...." I will always remember his words. "I am not ready for her to die."

Unity Library & Archives
1901 NW Blue Parkway
Unity Village, MO 64065

There was not a dry eye amongst the nursing staff that day. The tragedy of the moment was heightened by our recent success with exactly the same diagnosis and treatment of Amy. I remember thinking that I had to be strong for this family. It was very important for them to know that everything medically possible had been done, and that their daughter's life was now in God's hands. I may have even used those exact words, as I did in many similar situations, when I gave "the talk."

I remember standing at the foot of Cindy's bed in the crowded isolation room, made worse by all the monitoring and equipment in use, when Cindy's nurse, overcome by the emotion of the situation, placed her head on my shoulder. I reflexively placed my arm around her shoulders, and it was at that moment that I almost broke down. I did not let myself, however, because I couldn't allow myself that luxury. I had to get through this and move on. I had a PICU full of patients to care for, parents to talk to, and pediatricians to update. I could give these patients the strength they needed, but I couldn't afford to lose my own. My professional responsibilities would be compromised if I did. In short, my response to Cindy's death was a business decision.

Ironically, the nurses never saw it this way. They saw me as unique in my willingness and ability to deal with the families of dying children. It seemed that very few other doctors were so inclined. From my point of view, it wasn't that I had any particular gift; it was something I had to do. Dying children were an unfortunate aspect of my practice. To not deal with this effectively would have been to not do my job well and therefore become unpopular with nurses and families, thereby risking the success of my practice. It just so happened that I had established a way to deal with death that worked for me. It was effective, the nurses and parents seemed to respond to it, and it was of little risk to me.

Significantly, I managed without having to spend a lot of time delving into the meaning of death or understanding the process of dying or what happens to the soul. I had my religious beliefs about death and dying, but I spent little time reflecting upon or applying them to the situations of my patients' deaths. Dealing with death was simply another aspect of my practice, like treating asthma or negotiating with insurance companies. I faced death as best I could and then moved on to the next challenge of my practice, barely looking back for an instant. This was simply a refinement of the role I had established for myself while in training, with the added benefit of practicing good business.

There were times, however, when I was not completely immune to the miracle and mystery that surrounded some children's dying moments, no matter how hard I tried to minimize them. Take the case of Joey, a five-year-old who for two years had been battling an aggressive brain tumor that had wrapped around his brainstem. Because of its position and complexity, surgery was technically difficult, so Joey was placed on an aggressive chemotherapy regimen aimed at slowing the progression of the tumor. As in many chemotherapy protocols, one of the side effects was immune suppression. In other words, healthy white blood cells were killed by the toxins along with tumor cells, rendering the patient susceptible to opportunistic infections. A classic in this category is the organism Pneumocystis carinii, which causes severe pneumonia. It is one of the more common causes of pneumonia in patients with HIV disease because of the underlying immune suppression.

Joey was admitted to our PICU by his pediatric oncologist because he had pneomocystis pneumonia which failed to respond to aggressive outpatient therapy. He appeared to be in impending respiratory failure. Furthermore, because of his now life-threatening immune suppression, his chemotherapy had to be stopped, so his tumor was growing. By the time we received him, his outlook appeared hopeless. We gave him our best shot. He was placed on a ventilator, which was an emotional issue for his mother. Once intubated, he was no longer be able to verbally communicate with her. He was not yet old enough to write well, so she saw this step as the first one toward losing him completely. I explained to her that without placing him on a ventilator to more effectively deal with his lung disease we had little hope of pulling him through. We needed to at least give him a chance, and it was this argument that convinced her that it was worth the risk to lose contact with her son.

Even while Joey was on the ventilator, though, mother and son were able to find ways to communicate. He did a lot by pointing, nodding his head, and changing his facial expressions. There was very little that went unsaid, even between Joey and the staff, as long as his mother was at his bedside to act as interpreter.

We were fighting a losing battle, however. The bacteria had destroyed so much of Joey's lungs that there appeared to be little chance that we would ever wean him from the ventilator. Neurologically he began to deteriorate. He slept most of the time. When he wasn't sleeping he was in pain, which he demonstrated by a heart-wrenching grimace combined with large tears that ran down his cheeks. We used huge doses of narcotics to treat his pain. He had been on so much morphine for so long that he had built up an incredible tolerance. This made weaning him from the ventilator even less likely.

The day Joey died he had been in a coma for over twenty-four hours. His vital signs began to destabilize and I was worried that the tumor may have obstructed the flow of his cerebrospinal fluid, increasing the pressure on his brain. Left untreated this would eventually kill him. Joey was no candidate for surgery and his long-term prognosis was essentially nil. I explained all this to his mom and promised to increase his morphine to whatever dose it would take to keep him pain free. She agreed that we should not resuscitate him if he were to arrest.

Joey stayed alive through the next night, demonstrating to us an incredible degree of toughness and willingness to fight. Even his mother was impressed, although for the most part she was emotionally torn. She was not yet ready to lose her son, yet she could no longer stand to see him suffer. As she told me, she wished he could just die quickly and be in peace.

Invoking the memory of Alex, who had so many years before asked permission from his mother to die, I hinted to Joey's mother that the same dynamic may be occurring here.

"I know he cannot talk to us, but I believe he can hear us," I explained to her. "And I have seen situations where dying children hang on until their parents give them permission to die." I sensed her puzzled expression.

"You mean tell him it's okay to die?" She was truly confounded.

I explained, "Well, actually, yes!" I think I even smiled. "You are his mom. From you he seeks complete approval for everything he does…even dying." From her expression I felt encouraged to continue. "I have found over the years that the will to live is incredibly strong, often defying science." I was careful here—I didn't want to lead her to believe that there was any hope of recovery. "We know there is no hope, and I suspect so does he. At this point he is fighting to stay alive for you as much as for himself." I noticed tears welling up as she reached over to touch her unresponsive son's arm.

"So what do I do, Doctor?" She was nearly whimpering. "I only want to do what is best for him."

"I think it is okay for you to give him permission, to tell him it's okay to…die."

She unexpectedly fell into my arms and began to weep. It was extremely awkward for me, but I tried to comfort her as best I could. She asked for a moment alone with her son and I gladly agreed, relieved to escape from the emotionally charged atmosphere.

I don't know what she said to him in that room that day. I only know that within an hour of our conversation Joey was dead. That was the first time I recall thinking to myself more deeply about death and the soul. It was as if Joey had a sense of what was coming next and was not afraid. When Joey's mom left the room I sensed she no longer appeared frightened. Had they both come to possess some new knowledge? Were they taken to a place in their minds or souls that they recognized and felt comforted by? I even remembered wondering if they had somehow seen God in those last moments…yes, both of them. I never asked, though, because there was no way back then that I would have entered into that kind of intimate conversation with a patient.

In the end, Joey died as peacefully and painlessly as possible. So in essence I had done my job. Had he let himself be taken away because he had been given permission to do so? Did Joey and his mom have some glimpse of eternity that allowed them to be comforted by his death? I would never really know, and so I was only left to wonder. Little did I know how important these questions would become in the next few months.

CHAPTER NINE

Billy

During those early days of our fledgling PICU we performed some true miracles. I was proud of those cases, as was the nursing staff who worked so hard to make a name for our clinic in the community. A perfect example was that of a fifteen-year-old girl, Tina, about whom I received a call late one evening from the house pediatrician who was on duty. "We've got this girl," he had said shakily, "who has this strange red rash and she's well…." He paused.

"She's what?" I said curtly and somewhat rudely. Late night phone calls describing sick and deteriorating patients were then, and are still, one of the most difficult aspects of inpatient pediatrics. "What's going on with her?" I was practically shouting.

"Well, I can't get her blood pressure up. She's staying right at 60 systolic with a thready pulse."

"Is she awake?" I tried to get a feel for the situation, to

determine if I needed to go into the hospital or if it was something I could deal with from home.

"Yes, she's awake, and I've given her a fluid bolus. She doesn't look to be in any distress but she worries me, John."

About that, this young physician had been absolutely right. She definitely presented cause for concern. Shock in kids, even teenagers, is different than in adults. In adults, shock is almost always heralded by low blood pressure, even though physiologically it is much more complicated than that. Children, however, are so intrinsically healthy that blood pressure dropping in shock is one of the last things to happen, just before cardiac arrest and death. Shock is usually defined as the body's nutrient and oxygen supply unable to meet the tissues' demand. In other words, either the blood supply is inadequate to supply the tissues, or the tissues are behaving in such a way that their demand exceeds supply.

It turned out that Tina was a victim of toxic shock syndrome, which had only recently been adequately described when occurring in adolescent females. This syndrome is caused by a Staph bacteria associated with inappropriate tampon usage. The toxin released by the bacteria results in sepsis followed by shock and eventually multiple organ system failure. The mortality is high and treatment requires diligence and intensity. It is the quintessential critical care disease.

Tina survived after many days on the ventilator, multiple lines to monitor heart and lung function, intravenous nutrition and antibiotics—in short, by constant attention to every detail of her management. The nurses had done an incredible job, and I will never forget the night when my telephone rang at home and the nurses informed me they had someone there who wanted to ask me something. A weak, barely audible voice got on the phone and said, "I would like a pizza…" and then trailed off. It was Tina. She had spoken her first words after having been taken off the ventilator. She was on her way to recovery, and it was truly a triumph.

Years before I had treated a baby with severe pneumonia—who required several days on the ventilator, just as with Tina. Purely by coincidence, one day I happened to appear for rounds just as the nurses were having difficulty maintaining the child's blood pressure. It was a sudden and unexpected drop after the child had been quite stable and was being weaned from the ventilator. Just before this drop in pressure, the respiratory therapist had been suctioning the child's endotracheal tube, which required him to hand ventilate with ambu bag between suctioning passes. Apparently the bagging had been a bit excessive, forcing air to dissect out of the trachea into the mediastinum and eventually into the pericardium surrounding the heart. I did not know this until the chest X-ray showed up just as I was trying to determine the cause for the sudden blood pressure drop. Around the heart was the unmistaken image of free air indicating that the heart had been compressed down to the size of a small peanut. The blood pressure was low because the heart was being compressed by the free air; therefore, it was unable to pump effectively. If the air was not evacuated quickly, the child would die.

Applying essentially the same procedure I had used on that dying baby in the delivery room years before, I introduced a needle into this baby's pericardium. Thankfully, almost immediately the infant's blood pressure improved, along with her color and oxygenation.

These were the cases that made us proud and made us feel

confident that we could handle almost anything thrown at us. They were heady days. We were becoming a true PICU and we were doing it by saving lives…children's lives.

It was during this period that Billy came into my life. My strongest memory of Billy was that he was a beautiful child. He was four months old when I met him, having been admitted to the hospital by his pediatrician, who was concerned that he was not advancing properly through his developmental milestones. Initially he was admitted to the regular pediatric floor, but because the nurses were worried about his respiratory status and his ability to handle his secretions, they moved him into the intensive care unit where he could be monitored more closely.

When I walked into the unit Billy was laying in the open infant warmer; his mother, father, and the PICU nurse were at his side. At first I was struck by how calm he appeared, but then I realized that he wasn't moving at all. His eyes were wide open and he occasionally blinked. His mouth was partially open and his tongue appeared to be vibrating. His arms were at his side. His hands were still although his fingers moved ever so slightly. His legs did not move either, although his toes would wiggle from time to time. When I touched Billy's skin it was cool and dry and—this was the most impressive finding—incredibly soft. The softness is due to the lack of muscle tone of the subcutaneous tissues under the skin, which gives the skin an almost velvety feel.

Billy's face was angelic. It was round and soft. His eyes appeared huge and were surrounded by gigantic eyelashes. (I have come to notice over the years that kids with chronic, debilitating disease often possess long, luxurious eyelashes. I have never heard a good medical explanation for this phenomenon, but this finding has been borne out time and time again.) When Billy breathed his chest barely moved. Instead, his abdomen protruded out, and then back in again, in the characteristic "belly" breathing pattern of children with weak intercostal muscles.

It was clear rather quickly that Billy had a profound neurological disorder, and his lack of neuromotor development was due to the fact that his muscles were extremely weak. Even his respiratory muscles were barely sustaining him.

One of our first tasks was to obtain a neurology consultation. The pediatric neurologist immediately saw Billy and confirmed what we suspected: Billy's diagnosis was most likely spinal muscle atrophy, or Werdnig-Hoffman disease. This is a genetic disease usually passed on as a recessive trait, which means that both parents are carriers of the disease. This would become an important factor when it came to genetic counseling of Billy's young parents, who undoubtedly wanted to have more children. Children with this disease, which occurs sometime within the first two years of life, commonly receive a diagnosis of "floppy infant." The major muscles are affected and rendered essentially nonfunctional. At the time of Billy's diagnosis the life expectancy was about four years, and death usually occurred as a result of pneumonia and/or respiratory failure.

This was the news we would eventually have to deliver to Billy's parents. There was a hitch, however. The neurologist had performed a muscle biopsy which would reveal very specific findings if the diagnosis of SMA was to be made. We wanted there to be no mistakes in his diagnosis because the implications were too great, both for Billy and for any future siblings. The neurologist suggested that we send the biopsy to a laboratory accustomed to diagnosing SMA in infants. Because they saw a larger number of these samples, the possibility of error would be greatly reduced. The problem was that this would take time. The material would have to be mailed or couriered, then be examined, tested, and probably re-examined before an answer could be obtained. This result would then be sent to our neurologist, and finally the parents would be informed of the diagnosis.

I wasn't sure how much time we had before Billy progressed into full-blown respiratory failure, his little diaphragm unable to sustain the workload for his already weak respiratory muscles. Certainly any kind of respiratory infection might be enough to push him into failure, adding undue stress to an already weakened system.

The problem was this: although I had been frank with Billy's parents about the possibility of a severe, debilitating, progressive neurological disorder as his diagnosis, I had in no way been definitive. If he truly had Werdnig-Hoffman disease, as we suspected, his outlook was very grave indeed, and even with the ventilator, he would probably be dead before his fifth birthday. Without a ventilator, the slightest respiratory infection could kill him in a matter of days. Whether to intubate Billy in a respiratory crisis was ultimately up to his family. And their decision, I assumed, would depend almost completely on his diagnosis. But even a decision made on the basis of his diagnosis was not entirely clear-cut.

The more patients with chronic illnesses were near death, the less clear the decision was for me. If the diagnosis was positive, Billy would not live past his childhood even with respiratory support. His entire childhood would be on a ventilator, with a trach and probably a g-tube for feedings. He would never play or go to school. Billy would be able to interact, because the higher functions of his brain would be intact, but he would never talk and his interaction would be limited to eye movements and occasional finger movements. In essence, he would be a prisoner within his own body. Except for a functioning brain, he would have no meaningful physical function. Yet, there was no question that he could love and receive love. Unlike Michael and other patients whose brains had been ravaged by disease or injury, Billy would have very obvious and accessible emotions. On the other hand, his life would be limited and punctuated by periods of severe suffering and perhaps pain.

A large part of me, in those days, would have lobbied for not intubating Billy and letting "nature" take its course. I had seen too many kids suffer with severe disabilities and found it horrifying. No child should live his entire life on a ventilator, hooked up to tubes, needing suctioning and constant care, I would argue. That was not "life" according to my definition.

But then there were patients like Michael, who by most people's definition could be considered a vegetable, yet few children had been loved as much as he had. And if the measure of a person's life is the turnout at his funeral, then Michael had an incredibly successful life, despite his severe disabilities and brevity of time on the planet. It could be, I thought to myself, that Billy's parents would choose to intubate him, no matter what his diagnosis. I was not sure how I would feel about that. I was only sure of one thing: it should not be up to me to decide. Billy's parents needed to make the decision as to whether he should be placed on a ventilator or not, and they should make that decision with as much accurate information as possible.

The diagnosis seemed to take forever to come back. Each day I sweated it out with Billy. He was barely hanging on. He required almost constant suction, and the nurses were turning him and moving him around as much as they could to prevent the development of pneumonia. I was compulsive about the nurses who cared for him. They had to be the most diligent and dedicated, and they couldn't be caring for children with any kind of infection. The ultimate irony would be if he became infected in the hospital, an environment where he had been sent to be protected from respiratory compromise. But, as anyone who knows hospitals would attest, completely escaping infection is next to impossible.

As luck would have it—bad luck—Billy began to show subtle signs of a downward respiratory spiral. First he began to run a very low-grade fever, then his nasal secretions increased slightly. As his secretions worsened he vomited one of his tube feedings because he was unable to handle the formula along with his thick secretions. Slowly I watched his work of breathing increase. At first, we stayed on top of this by increasing his oxygen and the frequency of his respiratory treatments. These manipulations helped for a short time, but soon his seemingly relentless deterioration continued.

Finally the time had come to make a decision. I remember it being morning. I had been up half the night on the phone with the nurses trying everything I could think of to keep from having to place Billy on a ventilator. Once intubated, I knew he would be attached to the ventilator for the rest of his life. I hoped that by morning I would be able to get a definitive word on Billy's diagnosis and then his parents could make the best possible decision. But that word never came, at least not that day. As Billy slowly but inexorably slipped into respiratory failure, the scene in the unit was surreal. The moment had arrived when I had to intervene. I was having a difficult time keeping his oxygen saturation up, and he was truly struggling to breathe. Interestingly, because his respiratory muscles were so weak, extreme movements could not be noticed. But I could see it in his face. His little face, which had very little muscle strength even to convey emotion, told everything through his eyes, which had a look of panic. He seemed to be staring at me, pleading with me to do something. It was unbearable.

As I hovered over him at his bedside in the unit, two phone calls were being placed at the nurses' station. One was to our neurologist in a last-chance effort to see if the diagnosis had been definitively made. The other was to Billy's parents who, as luck would have it, already had decided to come in a little later that morning to spend some quiet time with him. Perhaps they sensed a decision point was approaching. Or maybe they were simply tired. In any event, they were not there at the moment when Billy and I needed them most.

We received word from the neurologist first: the diagnosis had not yet been made. Then the parents called. I would have to lay it all out for them as best I could, in as much detail as possible, but in as short a time period as possible before Billy went into full-blown respiratory arrest. I tried to remain calm and present the information in an objective manner without interjecting my opinion. But I had an opinion, a very strong one. I did not want to intubate this baby. I did not want to see those pleading, tired eyes looking up at me with a tube coming out of his mouth and eventually his neck, attached to ventilator. I did not want him to suffer infection after infection, hospitalization after hospitalization, enduring endless indignities, and then die anyway. As he looked up at me, with his eyes filled with terror, my temptation was to sedate him, take away his pain and discomfort and let nature take its course. Weren't some things worse than death? But it wasn't up to me.

I could not help thinking about Michael and his family, and before him little Jared. One family had chosen to end the suffering, while the other never even considered it as an option. Were both right? Did either love their child less? Was the end result for either any different? The only difference I could see was that one family had the opportunity to love their child longer; or did they? Did Jared's family's love or relationship end with death? I had more questions than answers, and knew only this: the parents would have to decide this one, and I would live with it; whether I agreed or not was immaterial.

When I was finally able to talk to them there was no decision to be made as far as they were concerned. As loving parents, their opinion was that they simply had to do everything medically possible until there was nothing more that could be done. So, of course I should proceed with placing him on the ventilator. In a way they were a bit surprised that I would even raise the question. When I sensed this from them I felt a little ashamed. I should never even have created this uncertainty in them. How could they have confidence in the medical care system if they sensed that the physicians disagreed with them philosophically? I mustn't ever question their decision again, I thought to myself. Undoubtedly, I would be seeing Billy for a while, possibly years, until there would be nothing more I could do for him. Things would go much better for all of us if Billy's family maintained trust.

Billy lived for two years on the ventilator before developing an overwhelming viral pneumonia that made it impossible to keep his lungs working effectively, even with the ventilator and maximal support. So we struggled with him for several days, using every ventilator available in the hospital, applying every setting and every modality. Nothing was working. His lungs became stiff and we were only able to maintain minimally acceptable oxygen levels. He had been in a coma-like state for a day or more, and soon we could expect his other organ systems to begin failing. His heart and kidneys were already beginning to show signs of dysfunction.

That last day sitting at Billy's bedside his parents reminisced to me about how much they had enjoyed him these many months… more time than they thought they would have when they finally learned that he had SMA. Had he been a normal child, he would have been walking, and jabbering up a storm. Billy manifested his development in other ways, they told me. He had become a connoisseur of books, devouring several a day. They read to him constantly, and he acknowledged the words with his wonderful eyes that compensated for all his other lost functions. His parents were becoming convinced that Billy actually had begun to learn to read, at age two.

Billy's parents said they were able to tell by his eyes when he found something funny because he laughed with his eyes. And they were also able to recognize his sadness, but Billy was rarely sad, they told me. In fact, there were many times when he had cheered them up. One look into his peaceful, happy eyes and they could be made to smile in an instant. They had indeed been blessed to have him, if only for a couple of years. And then they thanked me for saving him that day, two years earlier, and giving them the opportunity to love and enjoy him. In response to their thanks I simply said, "Don't mention it," and deep inside I wished they hadn't.

CHAPTER TEN

Alexis

In our effort to recruit subspecialists for our new Pediatric Intensive Care Unit, we came across some amazing individuals. One of those was a top-notch pediatric surgeon named Douglas Martin. At a fairly young age—he was in his late thirties—he developed an impressive reputation for surgical excellence at each of the two teaching institutions where he worked. Tired of the medical school bureaucracy, he was ready to try his hand at private practice. He heard of our program and was very interested in the opportunities it held for him. There was no question that we were in desperate need of a pediatric surgeon when he came along, and it was thrilling for us to land someone with such impressive credentials.

For Dr. Martin there were other attractions to our hospital. Douglas had recently married and his wife Karen was pregnant with their first child. He saw private practice as a way to have more control of his professional life, thus giving him more time to devote to his growing family. He also brought with him a whole new brand of medicine. He was dynamic, innovative, and unafraid of any challenge. Consequently, the volume of postoperative (and therefore sicker) kids increased.

It was an invigorating time for us professionally. The new PICU was thriving, and with physicians of Douglas' caliber we posed a threat to the university program, our competitor. By bringing him in, we moved into the next phase of our development: a force to be taken seriously. We began to receive the recognition we deserved from the pediatric community. Nurses were climbing over themselves to work in our unit, and the administration saw us as their golden child. Nothing, it seemed, could go wrong.

Alexis Martin's birth was a triumph in our program. In a way, it symbolized the "birth" of our new PICU, and our new flock of subspecialists. Her birth also made it clear that Douglas was willing to raise a family while working in our community and that he was here to stay. This was the sign of his commitment to our team that we had hoped for.

Douglas asked me to assist driving baby Alexis and Karen home from the hospital the day they were discharged, and I was excited by the prospect. My Cadillac was far roomier than his sports car, so his reason for asking me was purely practical. To me, however, this was much more symbolic: we were all part of the same family, brought together by this courageous experiment we embarked upon to take care of critically ill children in a private setting in a community hospital where we could provide the kind of high quality care we expected from all hospitals, whether private or university based.

Everything was about "the job" back then, even having babies. Douglas stayed home for the afternoon with his wife and Alexis. His mother-in-law was flying in later that day to relieve him. (He had cases in the operating room scheduled for the following day.) It was not that he was disinterested in his new daughter; on the contrary, he showed her newborn picture and bragged about her every chance he got. However, our jobs were "important." Every day children's lives depended on what we did in the PICU. Furthermore, the growth and reputation of the new PICU, our other "baby," depended on our total commitment and dedication. Wives, nannies and in-laws all pitched in with the raising of our own children so that we could focus our attention on our work.

There was a definite euphoria pervading the halls of our institution for several weeks following Alexis' birth. Perhaps it was a simple case of "when the surgeon is happy, everyone is happy." He was indeed happy, not in small part because of how long Karen had wanted a baby. From the impression they gave, it seemed that Alexis was their one chance, the only child they would or could ever have.

It was a cold Saturday morning in January when our phone rang at home. It was a beautiful day, one of those winter mornings when the wind is light, the air is crisp and clean, and the sky is royal blue. I had only one patient in the PICU that morning, made my rounds early, and had just completed an invigorating jog through the park. Pam, who had taken over the administration of our booming practice, was working in her office and our daughter was giggling softly with the babysitter in our basement playroom.

"Hello, John?" It was Douglas on the other end. I figured he was calling about a patient he wanted to put in the PICU, or some related matter. However, his voice lacked its usual energy and sounded rather distant.

"Hey, Doug, what's going on?" I was upbeat.

"It's Alexis…we're in the ER…." He paused as though something caught in his throat. "John, when we went in to check her this morning she wasn't breathing. Oh God, John, they've been coding her for an hour!" He was clearly crying now.

"Oh no, Douglas! What is it—what happened?" I was overwhelmed.

"SIDS, maybe, I don't know…they don't know…I had to put in the line for them."

SIDS, or Sudden Infant Death Syndrome, is one of the most horrifying illnesses for any parent. There is no known cause; it happens to children between the ages of six weeks and six months who have had no other previous illnesses. It used to be called "crib death," which is an apt description. Typically, a parent goes to check on their child first thing in the morning—often surprised that they have not yet made any noise—only to find them laying quietly in their crib, dead. All the medical knowledge and experience in the world is no defense against this tragic disorder.

It was inconceivable that this could have happened to this amazingly skilled pediatric surgeon. And the image of him placing a line in his own child, poking her with needles in a futile attempt to save her life, was incomprehensible.

"What can I do? Want me there?" Of course he wanted me there. I was at a complete loss for words.

"They want me to stop the code, John…I just can't do it alone and Karen is incoherent. She can't stop crying."

My God, I thought to myself as I tried to grasp the situation.

Their only daughter is probably dead at two months of age. Doug had to participate in the resuscitation, and now neither he nor Karen have the presence of mind to stop. I had become used to Doug making difficult treatment decisions in heated situations. When taking children in the operating room—sometimes not knowing what he might find—he was always poised, always cool, even in the most desperate situations. He was the person I called when I was in desperate situations with patients. And now he was calling me?

"John?" He called my name and I suddenly realized that I had been standing there saying nothing. "I need you here to help me make this decision. Please hurry."

Here it was then, the Ultimate Test.

I told Pam about the phone call. In a very cool and nonchalant way she made her way to the car. "We need to be there with them. Let's go."

That was all she needed to say to clear my head and get me going. Until she brought me back to reality, I was in a sort of suspended animation, not sure what I should do first. This was too real. This was not one of my patients. My usual mechanisms for dealing with things like this were not kicking in. Douglas didn't need me clinically; he needed me to be a friend, to comfort him in the loss of his child.

We arrived at the hospital in less than ten minutes, although it seemed like an eternity. Luckily, being a Saturday, traffic was not yet oppressive. I drove right up to the ambulance bay hoping a security guard wouldn't get in my way. The brisk air hit my face and helped to sharpen my senses. I was in a trance. The double doors opened and immediately the triage nurse pointed me to the closed doors of the trauma room. We could hear shrieking on the other side. As I opened the door, I spotted Douglas first. He was standing over the baby, openly sobbing. Karen was clutching him with both hands. A male nurse was halfheartedly performing chest compressions on Alexis, going through the motions of a ritual that had become pointless. The emergency room doctor stood quietly at the back of the room reviewing the code record with the charge nurse. Clearly, they had lost all capacity to deal with the magnitude of what they had been handed on that otherwise unremarkable Saturday morning.

As Pam and I entered the trauma room, Douglas and Karen nearly screamed. It was an unearthly sound. I shuddered and looked at Pam. We wanted nothing more at that moment than to run from the room. The pain was simply unbearable. There were no words; there was nothing that could relieve the reality we all faced. All they wanted us to do was be there with them; all we wanted to do was leave, go home and hug our own child. Why did we have this responsibility? Why did they want us? We were not family! This was not part of the expectation of our relationship.

But in truth we were family, brought together by the mission of caring for sick children. Now one of our own was sick, mortally so. But this wasn't supposed to happen to any of us! Of course rationally we knew it might, but in our hearts we could have never accepted our own mortality, and certainly not the mortality of one of our own children. The irony was only exceeded by the pathos. At that moment, in that ER, as we reassured Douglas and Karen that it was permissible to let the only child they would have together die, the business of caring for sick and dying children was no longer just business; it was now life, and that is the worst thing that can happen to a thriving business.

I went to the funeral in New England, in Karen's hometown. It was cold, clear, with a fresh blanket of snow. I was glad. The air needed to be cleansed, the ugliness covered. Pam stayed home with Elizabeth. I wish she had been there with me, but I was happy that she could be sheltered from the sadness. No matter how many times you see them, little baby caskets rip your heart out, and Alexis' did just that. Thankfully it was closed, but they had her baby pictures placed on top. Children's music played incessantly over the funeral home sound system, in place of the usual death music. It was really too much to bear—not just for me, but for many there.

Karen and Douglas were amazingly composed. Not letting go of each other, they walked through the room as if they were joined at the hip, like the Siamese twins Douglas had participated in separating during his training. I was struck by the oddity of their composure, just as I had been by that of little Felix's parents that first night of my residency. I was skeptical of the peace Doug and Karen emitted. It felt contrived, as if they were going through the motions but not really feeling it. I certainly felt no peace. And unlike the many deaths I had dealt with up to this point, this one was not going to go away when I left the room: I would be reminded of it every day when I saw Douglas' face. None of the mechanisms I used in dealing with dying children would work here. There could be no finality here, for this story was not yet over.

I stared out the window the entire flight home. The white blanket of January snow gave way to patches of brown and gray with hints of yellow. Rain-soaked roads crisscrossed the countryside as the plane descended into Louisville. What would happen now? We would all be changed, of that there was no doubt. But what would it mean for us, for our program? How could Douglas and I ever take care of a sick baby together and feel the same?

I left my car at the airport parking lot, the same stupid Cadillac I bought on a whim several months earlier but now hated for its flashiness—the same car Douglas had asked me to drive Karen and Alexis home in. Too bad it hadn't been stolen, I thought, because then I could get a new car, start over, change my image, in fact change everything.

When I got home the sun was setting. It was the time of day when people arrive home to their families, to the warmth of their homes, to the smells of dinner cooking, to the sounds of children laughing. I felt a little guilty for thanking God that I had all these things to come home to, and that the horror that ripped apart Douglas and Karen's life had not affected mine. Pam and Elizabeth were watching a Disney tape. Their smiles had never meant more to me. I had never felt more human, and less a physician. Were they really mutually exclusive? We hugged. Elizabeth giggled. And I cried, softly and persistently, for the first time since Alexis died.

I could not wait to get back to "normal," and neither could Douglas. Douglas now performed with a passion I had not seen before. I was a little surprised at how quickly he got back into the hectic pace of a busy surgery schedule and crowded clinics with rounds to be made. But I was glad for it because to me it meant that he was okay; he no longer needed me to be "a friend" in the mourning sense of the word. We could go back to the professional relationship we always had, one with which I was far more comfortable. Maybe we would get past Alexis' death faster than I thought. Maybe it wasn't that different from the other deaths I had dealt with after all.

Death to me meant "disappearance." Naturally it is sad when someone disappears, but with time we get accustomed to their absence and our sadness begins to fade. For me, patients who died in the hospital essentially "disappeared." That was the way I came to deal with them. Yes, there was sadness, but it was brief. The normal pace of life resumed as soon as I walked from a deceased patient's room.

Now, Alexis was gone. Of course we all missed her, but we were still here and there was work to be done. Further, we needed to figure out a way to live our lives without her, and do so as quickly as possible.

Karen didn't bounce back as quickly as the rest of us. She basically pulled herself out of circulation. Because she was out of our sight, she was also out of mind. Douglas rarely spoke of her, except when asked, and he invariably responded that she was doing as well as could be expected. Pam and I wondered about this, about how anyone could be doing so well after going through such tragedy, but we didn't question it, not as much as we perhaps should have.

We were unaware of how despondent Karen had become. Intensely proud, she did not want anyone to know the difficult time she was having, and neither did Douglas. She had stopped eating and became dehydrated, so much so that Douglas tried to treat her at home with IV's. But this approach wasn't successful. One night he came home late from the hospital and found her dead. Later he told me that he had not seen her appear so peaceful in months.

In my opinion, Karen died of a broken heart compounded by loneliness. In our collective inability to deal with the death of Alexis, we were not there for Karen. It wasn't that Douglas did not care about her anguish, for he loved her dearly. I maintain that he was limited by his profession. His experience taught him to deal with death as a doctor, not as a father or husband. His way of dealing with death? Reaffirm life, which to a physician means work. Work, unfortunately, leaves little time to care for anything else, especially a family member's pain, not to mention one's own.

CHAPTER ELEVEN

Bradley

After losing Alexis and then Karen, our PICU program, and family, never recovered. It was as though it had been touched by something contagious and evil, something so potent it affected all who were associated. Patients, nurses, pediatricians, and eventually most of us, fled like rats from a sinking ship. Finally the doors of the PICU closed, and to this day that hospital does not have pediatrics. "You couldn't take care of your own," the cosmos seemed to say to us, "so your team mustn't care for anyone in that institution."

Pam and I moved to a small community hospital outside of Tampa, where I went to help a sick friend who could no longer handle the clinical load. Luckily, that load was small, and the acuity did not seem high. In other words, it seemed as if the patients would not be too terribly sick. It was our job to care for any child requiring intensive care, or any patient in the emergency room that pediatricians or family practitioners felt uncomfortable with. It was the kind of medicine I liked, in a community that appeared benign and agreeable. Immediately, it felt safe.

Safe was a good way to feel since there was no question that we were, in fact, running away. We had our second child, Edwin, by this time. With two children in diapers, our practice in shambles, and our hearts confused, we moved to Tampa to start over. We were exiles, refugees. But rather than feeling persecuted we were relieved. My training was in caring for hospitalized children; it was too late in life to think about doing anything else. We were too confused to go to a part of the country we didn't know, and too beaten-up to tackle anything we didn't already know how to do. So we settled for the security of familiarity, a low profile, and hopefully an escape from tragedy.

For a time I truly felt as if we had left our troubles behind, as though a geographical healing had taken place. At that point in my life, I hadn't yet learned that one cannot escape from a problem that is essentially intrinsic. I was arrogant enough to believe that I could avoid dying patients rather than learn to deal with them. Moreover, I am now convinced that what one fears in life one also has a way of attracting. And what I feared most was death.

I knew I needed to overcome this fear, and that it would take time. For the short term, I needed an effective strategy that would keep me away from death yet able to work. Before Alexis and Karen died, I thought I had figured out a way of dealing with dying patients, but then when death hit so close to home even my expert defenses against dying patients collapsed. I needed to be in an environment where death was not such a certainty, where the patients were not so sick, at least not so much of the time.

Greenfield Community Hospital seemed to be the perfect fit. Unlike our situation in Louisville, at Greenfield we were not trying to be anything we weren't. In other words, we were a community hospital who knew its place. There was a core of very dedicated pediatricians in the neighborhood, and all they wanted was to be able to take good care of their patients. If their sick children needed to be admitted to the hospital and if, God forbid, they were sick enough to require intensive care, they simply wanted to know that there was someone on staff who could take care of them, and that there was a PICU where they could be managed.

The situation fit me like a glove. With two of us on call in a hospital where the patient acuity would be relatively low, the demand on my psyche was workable. We admitted one, perhaps two, patients per day, which was a very reasonable load. We saw many patients with asthma and other respiratory problems. Only occasionally did we have to put someone on a ventilator, and then for a very short time. There had been only one death in the PICU before I arrived: a child with many problems which led to a complicated surgery and an unfortunate postoperative course that resulted in a bad outcome. Although the staff had been shaken by this loss, because it was somewhat expected, their mourning was brief and left few scars.

Greenfield, I surmised, was a hospital where extremely ill children were a rarity, and therefore the staff did not need to emotionally prepare themselves for the possibility of death with every sick child they admitted, which was just fine with me. It helped considerably that there were three tertiary pediatric centers within transport distance from our hospital. Therefore, if we could predict that a child was going to be extremely ill, or if there were resources required that we simply did not have, we could transfer the child to one of these centers before his or her case became hopeless.

Unfortunately, within months of my arrival, my partner's health deteriorated and it became impossible for him to handle the long hours and uncertainty that went with being on call in the PICU. So he eventually left for the more controlled environment of the emergency room and its set hours, while I was left to carry the PICU alone. This meant being on call seven days a week, twenty-four hours a day.

In addition to the demands of caring for our pre-school age children, Pam became busy with the business aspect of our practice. We gave strong consideration to moving again, perhaps back to Louisville, or to a university setting where there would be fewer demands on our time. In the end, though, we elected to stay and deal with the devil we knew. A large part of our decision hinged on the fact that at Greenfield we felt insulated against tragedy. We had been wracked by the deaths we dealt with in Louisville, and knew we could never again face a similar environment. Here, we could be secure that we would be protected against such occurrences. I would be just one doctor, with a small but committed staff that had the authority to ship out any ill children who had even the slightest possibility of dying.

After my experiences with Douglas and Karen, I abandoned my professional mission to be the doctor "who handles death well." It appeared as if I was in the best position I had ever been in. I was able to practice intensive care pediatrics and avoid dying patients for the remainder of my career, or so it seemed.

By now it was now the summer of 1994. Summers were

typically slow for a community hospital such as ours. Our business was greatly affected by the respiratory virus season, which tended to be at its worst in the winter. So summers were left for more unusual diagnoses as well as trauma and surgeries.

On an otherwise typical summer night, the phone rang at about 2 A.M. On the other end was the familiar voice of an ER doc who said that he had been trying to page me for hours, which I knew was an exaggeration born out of his frustration and fear. I checked my pager. Indeed, the battery was low. I apologized and asked him what he needed. He said he had been "coding" an infant for over an hour and that he desperately needed me there to help him. I responded that I would be there in a few minutes, threw on my clothes, and drove to the ER as fast as I could.

It was easy to find my patient's bed by the crowd that had gathered. I immediately noticed one of our internists, Zack Brown, among the bedside crowd. This struck me as odd, since this partic-ular physician made it quite clear that he would not care for children unless it was absolutely necessary.

"It's my nephew." Dr. Zack Brown read my inquisitive expres-sion upon seeing him there at the bedside of an infant at 2 A.M. "Don't know what happened…think maybe she fell asleep while she was breast-feeding." His arms were crossed and his long, lean runner's body was crumpled ever so slightly, as if he was in pain. As usual, his words were few, which was his way, unless of course he was angry, which he might have been in this situation. After all, I had been late in responding and I was sure he knew that they had tried to page me several times. I had seen him explode before, but not in the irrational way of some docs. His outbursts were almost always justified, such as speaking up for a patient who had been given the runaround by radiology, or in response to a particularly ignorant decision by hospital administration.

Zack was not angry that morning. He was not angry because he knew what was happening: his six-week-old nephew was dying and he was powerless. Helplessness is a very difficult thing for doctors to deal with, especially when it comes to their own family. Douglas Martin dove in and took matters into his own hands by putting a central line in his own child, but that was unusual. Most reacted like Zack Brown, with silent resignation. He knew there was nothing he could do to save this baby; and most likely there was very little anyone could do. So he withdrew and left the infant's care to others who might have a chance. In fact, once I arrived on the scene he quietly slipped out, to comfort other family members.

Having children of his own, the situation was simply too much for Zack to handle. And I didn't blame him. It was at this point that it hit me as well: death had found me once again. I endeavored to run, but it followed me. The similarities to Douglas Martin's situation were frightening. Had it not been the middle of the night, and had I not been operating on a purely functional level, I would have been terrified. Was I being haunted? Was I Sisyphus, pushing the rock up the hill only to have it roll back to the bottom again? Clearly there was something I was not getting right, and history was going to be repeating itself until I did.

Zack Brown's little nephew died, and Zack's proposed cause of death proved to be accurate: the child's exhausted mother dozed off in mid-feed. Then the baby fell asleep and slipped down beside her. The mother's body, so well designed for feeding, comforting and nurturing, had in fact smothered the baby. The mother denied vehemently that this could have happened, which was to be expected. The guilt would have been tremendous, potentially insurmountable, no matter what the official cause of death.

For me, the experience was not as bad as it could have been. The family was incredibly close and supportive, and my new nurses, whom I initially thought of as naïve to such occurrences, proved to be a tremendous support for the family. They did not need me, it turned out, and I was relieved. So even though the Grim Reaper seemed to have followed me to this little hospital, perhaps there was a silver lining: maybe I wouldn't have to be on the front line dealing with the families of dying patients. Maybe this was a rare event, I told myself, an aberration. What a naïve denial! Before the summer of 1994 ended there were two more deaths, and my ability to deal with them was seriously tested…and I failed miserably.

That summer became legendary among the staff. In fact, we talk about it to this day. Sometimes we become philosophical about it. Sometimes they say that they are glad I was there or they never would have been able to deal with it. In my darkest moments, I think that summer happened because I was there with them; they were simply caught up in the nightmare of collateral damage I left along the roadways of my perverse journey.

The odd thing was that all three deaths happened very close together, within two or three weeks of each other in July and August, the "slow" time in pediatrics.

The second death was that of a baby just under three months old who was found dead in its crib. The age and scenario was classic for SIDS, and the family knew it. The only reason the child came up to the PICU from the ER was that the resuscitation had been successful enough to restore heartbeat, but there were no spontaneous respirations or neurologic function. Our job was to go through the criteria for declaring brain death, and then hope that the family would agree to make the child an organ donor. An infant heart was very difficult to find, and at that time heart transplant was the only possible treatment for some congenital cardiac disorders.

This was good for me. It gave me something to focus on when talking to the family. Since I could spend time educating them on the procedure for declaring brain death and organ donation, I didn't have to spend time on the far more difficult but no less real issues like death, dying, loss, mourning and, God forbid, the soul and eternity. I was nowhere near ready for this, nor did I ever plan on becoming so. I had pretty much decided to stay away from issues I either didn't understand or those that were based more on emotion than intellect. From now on I would leave such things to clergy and supportive family members, just as I had with Zack Brown's nephew. Besides, I rationalized, they were far better equipped than I was so did a much better job. Thus I enabled myself to avoid feeling the family's pain. It seemed to me to be the only way I could survive this curse.

I was thankful to have very factual issues to discuss with this family. For me, it was painless. It was a win-win situation, and to my amazement this strategy worked! We were able to establish that the child was clearly brain dead, and the parents even agreed to make the child an organ donor. I remember the father thanking me for our kindness and compassion, and for helping them to realize that although it was terrible that they had lost their baby, their child's organs could be used to restore life in another.

Had I stumbled on a new and improved method of dealing with death? Would I call it the "just the facts, ma'am" approach to talking with family members about their dying children? Families expected me to talk to them, and it appeared that it mattered not what I talked about, just so long as I went to the bedside and talked about something. I vowed that the next time a child died, I would find something about the case that I felt comfortable discussing and stick to that. More painful issues, like death itself, I would outsource to others. Thankfully, our nurses seemed to have a wonderful knack for comforting grieving families. I had no idea what they said, or how they approached heartbroken families. I didn't want to know. They did it well, and that was all I needed…until the third case of the summer came along.

Bradley was an eighteen-month-old boy, the picture of healthy early toddlerhood. He had recently learned to stand unassisted and was on the verge of taking his first solo steps. His mother was a single parent and a successful businesswoman, so Bradley had a babysitter who was trusted like a family member. One day, during Bradley's afternoon nap, the babysitter went in to check on him and discovered that he wasn't breathing. He had managed to get himself tangled in a comforter inside the crib, which must have suffocated him, the babysitter surmised. The quick-thinking sitter untangled Bradley from the comforter, performed CPR and rescue breathing, and restored him to normal. She then called 911, who dispatched EMS immediately. The child was taken to the emergency room at our hospital for evaluation. That was when I first received a call from the ER physician.

"John, we have this kid here who stopped breathing at home," the familiar voice said to me. "His sitter did CPR and he wasn't down too long. He looks great now, so I called his pedi and she asked me to give you a call to see what you thought."

"Wow," I started my learned discourse. "Did the child have a seizure or something? I mean, what happened to him?"

"Well, his sitter found him wrapped in some kind of blanket, but I don't know if that explains it. We thought we should run it by you."

I was a little perplexed. Bradley was beyond the age for SIDS, the same mysterious disorder that had taken Alexis Martin. The blanket could have been the explanation, but a child Bradley's age should have been able to fight his way out of it. Having seen my share of child abuse, I considered foul play but resisted thinking about it any more than I had to.

"Let's admit him anyway," was my answer. "This way we can hook him up to monitors and just sort of keep an eye on him. Maybe get an EEG or something."

"OK, if you say so." He was a little surprised. "He looks really good though."

"I know, but it never hurts to admit, just in case."

And that was all there was to it. He was sent up to the PICU and was the only patient there that night. We hooked Bradley up to full monitoring and watched him.

It was Bradley's mother from whom I got the history that evening. She was a very nice woman and we established a good rapport. What she recounted to me was a description of Bradley's unremarkable medical history in his infancy and childhood. She was understandably nervous about what had happened to him, especially since we didn't have a definitive explanation, so she was comfortable with our keeping him for an overnight observation.

Bradley's night was completely uneventful, so we discharged him the following day without incident. I talked with Bradley's mother for quite a while before she left, reassuring her that although this event was frightening, Bradley seemed to have suffered no ill effects and should do just fine. As to the cause, I told her the only reasonable explanation involved the comforter and therefore she should remove it from the crib. Once this was done, there would be no chance of this ever happening again. "Just go live your lives!" I think were the somewhat prophetic words I used when I discharged them, everyone smiling and happy.

One thing I did not talk to her about was child abuse, attempted murder. There had been cases in the medical and lay literature about suspected cases of SIDS that were actually homicides in the form of smothering. Infants and toddlers demonstrate few physical signs of injury when suffocated, even on autopsy, except by very trained observers. The thought crossed my mind that this could have happened to Bradley. There were scenarios where mothers caused harm to their children and then rescued them in order to get attention either from other family members or the medical establishment. Could this have been Bradley's babysitter's motivation? There was no way I could have known. And after talking at length with Bradley's mom, who emphatically stated how much she trusted and appreciated this babysitter, I couldn't bear to suggest that someone she held in such esteem might be a potential murderer! So I said nothing.

I did, however, give Bradley's mom my pager number so she could contact me directly if Bradley did anything unusual, or if she had any other questions. To this day I don't know why I did what I had never done before! My pager was just for staff, never for parents. I must have had some lingering uncertainty that even I wasn't consciously aware of, something that made me want to be available to her.

Two days later my pager went off. It was Bradley's mom. She informed me that Bradley had "done it again," only this time the sitter was not able to bring him back. The ambulance was en route and she was on her way from work to meet the ambulance, and asked that I do the same. I was already in the ER when it rolled in.

Bradley was on the stretcher, intubated, and the EMT was bagging him. A second tech carried his IV fluids with one hand, while he pushed the stretcher with the other. They pushed him into the pediatric trauma area and lifted him onto the bed. I remember trembling as I looked at him. The sparkling, smiling face I had seen only two days before was now pale and lifeless. His skin was cold, his pulse thready. CPR had restored his heartbeat but his blood pressure was minimal. I placed my hand on his forehead which felt slightly warmer than his extremities. I used my thumb and forefinger to pull back his eyelids. His eyes did not move and his pupils were dilated. I took the otoscope light from the wall and shined it directly into his eyes. His pupils did not respond. I remember saying to myself at that point, "Someone smothered this child."

Another brain-dead baby, the third in as many weeks. This one was the worst of them. Bradley was one of our patients. We knew him! We had already taken care of him when he was alive. No one was prepared for this, least of all me. Like the previous case, we would have to go through brain-death procedures, and then attempt to designate him an organ donor. How could I discuss these issues as easily as I had the previous time?

I had reassured this mother that nothing like this would ever happen again, but it did, only much worse! I was sure it was murder and so was everyone else in the hospital that night, including the Sheriff's department, which seemed to be everywhere. How could I tell her this? Worse yet, how could I avoid discussing this with her? There was no way I could bring myself to do it. Discussing death was one thing, but telling a distraught mother you think her child might have been murdered? Impossible! Was it really my place? After all, I was a mere physician, not a forensic specialist. Even the medical examiner wouldn't commit himself as to the cause of death.

The police certainly had their hunches and discussed these with the mother. But there was no hard proof. The babysitter's story remained the same: She checked the child at the same time, and under the exact same circumstances as two days earlier. Once again, she found Bradley not breathing. Everyone knew what happened, but no one could prove it, so nothing was said.

A year later Bradley's mother sued me. She felt there was some medical reason for his death that I had failed to diagnose, and she had plenty of experts to support this theory. We had no evidence to support our contention that he had been smothered, other than circumstances. So, my insurance company lost lots of money which went mainly to attorneys, and then they classified me as an insurance risk and dropped me. I have struggled ever since with this black mark on my credentials, but this is nothing compared to what Bradley's mother had to struggle with, and largely because I didn't talk to her frankly and compassionately about her son's death. Not that I could have prevented it, but I have spent many sleepless nights wondering if I could have. Finally, I concluded that I couldn't have.

Given the facts I had during Bradley's first admission, there was nothing else I could have done to prevent his death. My own fears, however, contributed to the final outcome. Had I been able to deal with his death, I could have supported his mom at the time when she needed answers and comfort. But the truth is, I was not there for her. Did this contribute to my being sued? I have little doubt. To this day I would welcome the chance to discuss the case with her without lawyers, without medical examiners, and without the debilitating fear that enveloped me that horrible summer.

Mercifully, the summer of 1994 ended, but not before leaving death, destruction, and depression in its wake. After Bradley, I truly wanted to quit, to give it all up. I thought I could avoid death at Greenfield, but I was very wrong. It followed me there and then reared its ugly head with a vengeance I had not yet experienced. I had thought I could figure out a way to deal with it, an operational method for keeping myself away from the pain while yet helping its victims deal with theirs. I was wrong about that, too. Avoiding pain does not diminish it. Quite the contrary, so I have learned.

Meanwhile, I had responsibilities. I was a father, a husband and a provider. I needed to remain reliable...and sane. I had chosen the life that accompanied my profession. It involved death; it always would. I had to hang in there and stop feeling sorry for myself. Perhaps if I just kept at it, I mused, answers would come. But please, God, let them come without any more death!

CHAPTER TWELVE

Janice

Survival became the key operating principle for Pam and me after that horrible summer of 1994 with its lawsuit and subsequent fallout. My family became my refuge. Pam, as always, was my strength. Time and time again, when I was feeling particularly desperate about my situation, she reminded me that I do what I do because I am so well suited for the job. In an attempt to comfort me, she often said that my patients were lucky to have someone who cared so much and worked so hard for them. Although it was nice and reassuring to hear those words, what I had a difficult time articulating to her was that it was fear that made me so good. Fear was, in fact, my prime motivator. My hope was that my fear would help me to perform in ways that would keep me out of trouble. The term "defensive medicine" was an understated cliché for what I was practicing in those days.

I dreaded each admission, each call from the ER, every request from a pediatrician to care for a child he or she wanted to admit to the hospital. Would this be the next one who would die on me? What hidden disaster awaited me if I admitted this child? I did my best to make sure that everything went well and that everyone was happy. I was insanely compulsive about checking and rechecking. Nurses sometimes wondered if I had lost my mind. Parents sometimes worried because I was giving them too much attention. "There must be something horribly wrong," they surmised, "or why else would this doctor keep checking on my child?"

Ironically, this behavior gave me the reputation of being a very competent, conscientious and caring physician. Had they known my true motivation, they would have been somewhat less generous with their praise. It was true that I wanted only good to happen for these children, and certainly I couldn't stand for another of them to die. So I did everything humanly and medically possible to prevent that from happening. I talked to parents incessantly, informing them of every aspect and every possible outcome of their child's illness. I didn't want any surprises and I didn't want them to have any surprises that might come back to haunt me later.

Paradoxically, as my reputation as a caring physician grew, I felt as if I was getting ever closer to the edge. I was so sure that another death or another surprise outcome would do me in. I compensated with near pathologic compulsion. I once saw a sign in front of a church that reminded me of the way I practiced medicine which read: "Others see our methods, but only God sees our motivation." No one knew my motivation back then and it didn't matter; it was results that mattered, no matter how they were achieved.

To this day, when I am on call I sleep very little, especially if I have a patient in the PICU. I regularly phone the nurses the very last thing before I go to sleep, and then again the first thing after I awaken. I am known in our unit for my 5 A.M. phone calls, and occasionally am the brunt of jokes because of this behavior.

When I wasn't working it was my own kids that kept me busy. By this time they were both in school and life had taken on the controlled chaos of the post-modern, too busy suburban household. With Pam's billing business in the home she seemed to be working constantly. The kids had a fairly structured day, but its demands required us to always be prepared and "on." Since I had no partners I was on call all the time, which meant I was completely at the mercy of the hospital. If anyone needed me, I was there. The minute things quieted down just a little, I left to help out with the busy home schedule. I did what I could with the kids, but much of the time I was simply going through the motions. Pam sometimes asked me, "Where are you?" It wasn't difficult to know what she meant by this rhetorical question. I was a zombie, the walking dead. Life was about moving robot-like from one thing to the next, doing the many tasks that were before me. I executed them without emotion, because emotion could hurt, and I had enough hurt. Unfortunately, however, when you eliminate hurt you also eliminate the possibility of joy. But I had had enough highs and lows. My present goal was to survive.

As I think about it, it was the perfect scenario for substance abuse. Sometimes I am convinced that the only reason I didn't begin drinking excessively or searching out other forms of chemical escape was that I was just too busy, too tired, or too deep in denial of the emptiness I felt. But my aspirations were not lofty:

I wasn't looking for joy or satisfaction, just let me survive in a healthy enough state to keep working and to care for my family, was my prayer.

Pam had an older sister, Janice, who in many ways was the sister I never had. She and Pam were the two middle children and alternated in manifesting the middle child syndrome. This gave each of them a unique feistiness and independence, which became the cause of their individual successes in life. They grew up poor, so were deprived of even basic cultural experiences. The scars from their childhood were deep. Their father, an itinerant shrimper, was unabashedly unfaithful to their mother and pursued his affairs with complete lack of discretion. Eventually their family had to leave town in order to escape the ill will he had created in the wake of his affairs. Their mother lived in a constant state of shame, which blunted her ability to unconditionally love or feel love. She lived a life of subsistence, dwelling on the things she could provide—food and shelter—while falling short in providing her children with the basic nurturing they required.

Janice and Pam had each other, and their love and support for each other was unconditional. The bond they developed as self-protection in childhood continued into adulthood. Together they dealt with their past with humor and a shared strength. The worst of their childhood became the best of what they were together. They had the kind of relationship where communication was multileveled and profoundly honest. When they were together they sparkled. It was as if they were proud of what they had overcome to become the people that they were.

Janice not only went to college, she went twice. After obtaining a bachelor's in nutrition she lost interest in this field so went back to school to get an electrical engineering degree. With this she became one of the few females of her era who worked as a civilian for the Navy at their installation in Panama City, Florida.

Although Janice's professional life was subject to the discipline and order of the Navy, her personal life was all about having fun. She was one of those people who thought we deserved to have fun whenever possible. We all worked hard, she used to tell us, and when the work was done we deserved to enjoy life.

Her passions were wine, running, and sex. She and her first husband knew everything there was to know about wine and were superb long distance runners. He was never able to keep up with her passion for sex, however, and this became a sore spot between them. When they were with us, however, there was little evidence of tension. Pam and I enjoyed being around them because their joie de vivre had a way of rubbing off on us and made life joyful. They never had children, and I remember when Pam and I were first married—partly influenced by Janice and her husband—we swore that we would remain childless as well. We sacrificed enough already, we told ourselves, and besides, the world was too evil to introduce to children.

Janice was the social organizer of our extended family. For any holiday it was she who decided where we would all get together, what we would eat and drink, and how we would amuse ourselves. The rest of us went along for the ride, amazed at her initiative and creativity. At a time when our lives were filled with work, duty, commitment and responsibility, she gave us the diversions we so badly needed. Her love of life was infectious. It was Janice's primal need to laugh, to enjoy food and drink in one another's company, that brought our family together at times when very little else would have. She kept us in touch with parts of life we continually denied ourselves. Janice made you want to be near her, like a wonderful sister who loves you completely, including your flaws, fears, foibles, and all.

Janice and Pam talked about everything. Although we lived several hundred miles apart, when our relationship was at its closest we saw each other regularly. Janice and Pam accumulated enormous phone bills. When Pam had our babies, it was Janice who made the trip to be with her. She cooked great meals for us and begged us not to forget to have fun. It was her mantra, which sometimes we condescendingly mocked. There were other times, however, when we embraced her hedonistic tendencies with vigor.

Janice's first husband was over ten years older than she. We postulated that they married because he represented a substitute for her poor fathering. While this theory was pop psychology at its worst, its conclusion was too painfully obvious to ignore. Her husband enjoyed life as well, which was the foundation of their relationship. After many years of marriage, however, she tired of him and the old-man ways into which he began to slip. His need for sex never matched hers, and she was quick to complain about his lack of imagination in such matters. To her, sex was as important to the daily enjoyment of life as good red wine or gourmet food. You might be able to live without it, or with a cheap substitute, but what, then, would be the purpose of living?

Eventually they divorced, and we were kept abreast of every step of their marital breakup. I would have liked to have remained friends with him, but it seems to be traditional that the blood relative receives allegiance in a marital split, even when there exists sympathy for the position of the other party.

Janice spent several years single. She was approaching her forties by this time, but easily looked ten years younger. She became passionate about running and fitness, and her crowning glory was the completion of the Boston Marathon in 1991.

Her running produced an incredibly lean and muscular physique. She let her strawberry blonde hair grow long, and indulged herself in some plastic surgery which gave her the air of a confident, mature twenty-seven-year-old. Soon she was the talk of the Navy base and her social life sky rocketed.

Pam and I were taken through the ups and downs of her many relationships. Janice never enjoyed being single though, at least not for long, and soon we began to hear more and more about Jack, a man in whom she developed an increasing interest. He was slightly older than she, but the age difference was not as extreme as it had been with her first husband. We met Jack several times before they were married. Although he seemed pleasant enough around us there was something about his eyes or perhaps his forced smile that made us uncomfortable. Pam and I discussed these feelings often and discounted them as being typical of the family members about the "second" husband. Still, there was something.

Janice sensed our apprehension and did not appreciate it. Distance and tension increased between us. Janice loved our opinions on her life, but she never wanted to be told how to live it. She and Jack had a tumultuous relationship, but she spared us certain details, attempting to avoid our inevitable disapproval. When they were in the midst of an argument Janice would call Pam either out of loneliness or anger, and she spoke of Jack with the utmost candor. There was one particular event that, although frightening to us, should have scared us more and forced us into action. In retrospect, I think it was our sense that Janice didn't want to include us in every detail that kept us from getting more involved. Or, perhaps this is just my rationalization for the guilt I felt for not trying harder to intervene.

Before long, Jack became possessive of Janice. His insecurity was somewhat understandable given the fact that he was an ordinary appearing guy, while Janice had become the talk of the Navy base. Possessing her was the achievement of his lifetime, and keeping her became his obsession. They had heated arguments, many of which centered around Jack's inability to meet Janice's demands for sexual satisfaction. We advised her that disputes in this area were very sensitive, so when dealing with a man's sexual prowess one must tread very gently. She listened to our advice, but soon returned to her overriding opinion that if she was his woman, then she deserved to be satisfied by him and had every right to demand such satisfaction no matter what it took.

During one particular altercation wherein Jack was no doubt put on the defensive, he began to feel that their relationship was in jeopardy. When he reached a point where words were no longer effective in convincing Janice of his devotion to her, he got his revolver and brought it into the kitchen. He put one bullet in the chamber and held the barrel to his head, threatening to pull the trigger if he thought he was going to have to live without her. Later, he took her to an isolated place in the woods where he would go to "think," as he told her. Once again, he took out his revolver and acted out his version of Russian roulette. When she promised that she would not leave him they made love right there on the floor of the woods, the handgun within reach, an act which horrifies me to this day.

These manipulative tactics worked, and the arguments soon ended; however, Janice's dissatisfaction with him did not. When she told Pam about these incidents, even more striking than the actual events was Janice's reaction to them. Sure, she had been frightened, but not enough take action. In fact, soon after they were over, she made light of them, drawing symbolic connections between guns and penises. It would have been uncharacteristic of her to react any other way. Any difficult point in life could be gotten past, she would often say, so that we can more quickly get back to the good parts.

When Pam told me about the Russian roulette incidents I broke into a cold sweat. Having always been petrified of guns anyway, I couldn't help but remember an argument I once had with Janice regarding personal handguns for "self-defense." It was my contention that guns in the home were responsible for more killings of family members than of bad guys. Her counter was that she had the right to defend herself and therefore to keep a gun in her home or carry one in her purse. We had many such arguments over the years, during which both of us would become passionate and unyielding in our respective positions and end by agreeing to disagree.

I eventually told Pam that she needed to demand that Janice remove every gun from her home. I further informed her that I didn't care what it would do to our relationship with Janice and Jack, but from that day forward I would never have my children at any function where Jack was also present. Pam, with surprisingly little argument, agreed.

To our dismay, not only did Janice stop listening to us—and to a large degree stop communicating—but she married Jack in a civil ceremony marking the beginning of the end of our relationship.

It was February 1996. I had a partner by then and life had begun to take on a comforting rhythm. Since I was not on call every day, I was able to temper my fear-provoked burnout with welcome time off from the PICU. It was a simple yet brilliant solution for what was a potential catastrophe. Had I not found help when I did, there was no way that I could have lasted. It was no longer a question of whether or not I enjoyed my work; I was scared to death of it. The only treatment that I knew for this condition was to get away from it as much as possible, hence the partner.

So, on the days when I was off from the PICU, it was my job to wake, dress, feed and take the kids to school, so that Pam could concentrate on her work in her home office. I loved Florida winter mornings. There was a feeling of liberation as I walked the kids to their classrooms. Ed was in kindergarten by then and was sometimes reluctant to leave us for school; however, with a little reassurance he always went. I left them comforted by the knowledge that they would be safe for the day. I drove along Bayshore Boulevard in Tampa, taking in the bay reflecting the incredible azure sky, listening to music, or talk radio, or whatever! The terror of the PICU could not affect me. I was sheltered from death and despair, even if it was only for that day, which was enough. My spirit was recharged and replenished, allowing me to face my time on call again. It seemed as if our family had reached a level of equilibrium. It was not perfect, but it worked, and with time we might even heal.

It was Wednesday, and I shall remember it always, not just for the horror that sliced its way into our lives, but also for the tranquility it rudely interrupted. The contrast made the evil even more acute, and at first nearly impossible to accept.

I had just returned home from my school trip and attendant errands. I went to the upstairs level of our townhouse to greet Pam and go through our morning ritual of giving "report" when the phone rang. I took that as my cue to head back downstairs to reheat some leftover breakfast coffee. Suddenly, the low rumbling of Pam's voice was punctuated by one of the most bloodcurdling shrieks I had ever heard, especially from Pam. I ran up the stairs and down the hall to her office. When I entered the room, her face was contorted, the phone precariously dangling from her ear. Her typically pleasant countenance was replaced by an expression I had never seen…a mixture of fear and hate and horror and a kind of life-shattering disappointment.

"Janice is dead," she announced, and I myself nearly collapsed. Yet, in an eerie way I was not totally surprised. I have spent years trying to understand how I could have been simultaneously horrified yet not completely astonished. Some of it had to do with my feelings about Jack. In a way, Janice's last days were like waiting for an impending execution: you know exactly what is going to happen, and even when, but when it finally does happen it is still shockingly horrific.

Their bodies lay side-by-side on the floor of the master bathroom of the house they had just bought as a wedding present to each other. The gun was under Jack's body, which is how the police determined he did the shooting. It was the revolver that they kept in their bedroom, in the top drawer of his dresser, easily accessible in the heat of an argument. That day, after they each had several glasses of wine followed by loose talk of his sexual performance—along with Janice's threat to leave him again—he decided that if he couldn't have her, no one could.

After eating the steak dinner Janice prepared for him, Jack opened the yellow pages to the funeral home section while she was in the bathroom putting on her makeup. Her view in the mirror was at such an angle that she no doubt saw him approaching with the gun, which he then put to her temple. BANG! It was all over. Like road kill before it becomes road kill, she saw him pull the trigger. He then took the lipstick from the counter and wrote the date and time on the mirror, stood over her, pointed the gun at his forehead, and then fell dead beside her. It happened on a Sunday afternoon, but the bodies were not found until late Tuesday, when they each had missed two days of work.

Of the many things discussed in the aftermath of Janice's murder was Pam's worry that Janice may not have had time to "make her peace," as she put it, before she died. Janice had never been religious, and was openly agnostic much of her life. But Pam felt her sister probably thought of God in those last few seconds. And in a cruel irony, the fact that she must have seen Jack coming at her in the mirror may have given her just enough time to take stock of her life. Believe it or not, it was things like that that we took solace in during the darkest of our days.

To say that our life came crashing down upon us would be the grossest of understatements. We were a beachside shack falling victim to a hurricane. We were not just taken apart, we were obliterated, flattened with little hope of being reconstructed. It is not an exaggeration to say that had it not been for our children we would not have been able to go on. Pam admitted to me some time later that she actually gave a passing thought to suicide. The futility of life overwhelmed us. However, we had a strong sense of responsibility for our children. God knows we were sometimes responsible to a fault. In the winter and spring of 1996, it was precisely that sense of responsibility that overcame all other motivators and kept us alive.

For me, Janice's death had its own unique impact. Once I got over the immediate effects of something so horrific happening to a family member, a second wave of terror set in: death had sought me out and followed me once again. This time it wormed itself into my family, a place I had previously thought was sacrosanct. My attempts to avoid it had not only failed, it was as if I was being punished for trying to avoid it. I became paranoid and began to think that I was being tortured. If I did not accept death, it was going to keep stalking me, closer and closer, even involving the people I loved, until I gave in to it. But I couldn't. My reaction was still to run, to avoid, to escape further. When fear is your prime activator, escape is your operative defense mechanism. But how much further could I go before I lost everything? How could I hide and still live, provide for my family, raise my children, take care of my patients? I felt consumed by darkness with little hope for light.

CHAPTER THIRTEEN

Sheree

Most of humanity lives in the little picture. Each of us lives day-to-day, sometimes hour-to-hour. We plan for what will please us, for what will bring happiness this week or this month, or perhaps next year. We avoid the big picture because we don't understand it, and because we don't understand it we fear it.

After Janice's murder, clinging to the little picture gave Pam and me our solace; it was the only sense of security we had; it was all that we could control. When raising small children it is very easy to get lost in the minutia of daily living, those endless details that make up a day. A misstep in any of those details and the day could become a failure. These tedious details were a godsend for us. Without them we would have been lost in our own depression. There was no denial whatsoever about our depression, which we readily admitted to each other. The blessed duties of everyday living provided a welcome distraction. Besides having children to rear, we had a medical practice and a business to run. If we dared to stop, so would our little world, and everyone who depended on us would be affected. Thank God for the little picture!

The messy business of death became a haunting distraction. With all the deaths I had experienced in the PICU, I had been spared the complications that families confront following a death: property, possessions, debts, insurance, employment and, of course, legal issues (with the exception of a wrongful death lawsuit which cannot be termed a simple detail). It was not that there had been no deaths in the family; for in fact, aunts and uncles in my hometown in upstate New York, who were much older than my parents, had begun to die. I was close to many of these people growing up, but when I left home for medical school and residency training I all but renounced my childhood attachments. So when those who had been close to me during my childhood began to die, I no longer felt a strong pull to return to pay my last respects. Of course I had great excuses: I lived far away; I was on call all the time; my children could not travel…whatever. The truth is that I really didn't want to be part of the death experience. I was barely getting by dealing with the emotional strain of caring for critically ill children and watching them die with some regularity. The raw reality was that I had already figured out how to deal with those deaths, whereas within my own family there would be "details" to discuss—an aftermath to the death—which was simply too much for me to bear. The fear I felt then and the moments I missed supporting family during those miraculous times are lost forever, and I will be forever regretful.

In contrast, avoiding the "details" of Janice's death was

impossible. We were her closest relatives. Pam was her personal representative, so there was no option. Death and its aftermath had to be faced, and faced head-on.

Janice was not a wealthy person. Her freewheeling lifestyle was not compatible with savings, so naturally she had none. She was, however, well employed and had good credit. She had good insurance, an expensive home with nice furnishings, all of which became disputed territory, made worse by a murder-suicide scenario. The ugliest aspects of human nature were revealed on all sides and no one was happy. Ironically, Janice would have wanted everyone to be happy, even sorting through the debris of her life, and she probably would have thrown a party to be sure!

When Pam first brought up the issue of Janice's possessions I immediately recoiled with horror. "I don't want anything that was part of that horrible home," was my self-righteous reaction. Pam was disappointed in me. My insensitivity allowed no awareness of the memories of Janice that were attached to her belongings. I wanted to get past it all as quickly as I could. Her possessions would only be reminders of all that I wanted to forget.

I became acutely aware of just how important personal items are the day I found Pam sitting on the floor of our attic storage room surrounded by Janice's running awards—trophies, ribbons, posters—quietly crying as she surveyed them. When she sensed me watching her she became self-conscious and tried to hide her tears. "What a waste…" was all she kept muttering, shaking her head and letting the tears flow onto the trinkets that represented her sister, her best friend's proudest moments on earth.

At work I was in zombie mode, devoid of emotions and avoiding interpersonal contact at all cost. Whenever patients were unstable I did everything possible to remove myself from the case. What a total contrast to the earlier days of my career when I relished the tough cases and felt the rush of the challenges of diagnosis and the excitement of managing a child with one or more organ system failing.

But not now, not anymore. When a sick child might die, there was no way I could face it. The nurses noticed and began to wonder. Very few knew about Janice—not that it was some horrible family secret, I just didn't want to talk about it with them or anyone. I wanted the hospital to remain the one place on earth that I could control. Without Janice's memory there I imagined I was somehow safe. Of course the nurses needed some explanation for my bizarre change in behavior and eventually found out its cause. They never told me they knew, they just tacitly accepted what I had become and hoped that eventually my former self would return so that we could take care of patients the way we always had.

Actually, my former self was never to be heard from or experienced again. In its place there emerged a new and improved version, one that defeated fear, accepted death, and embraced life. But it took a miracle to make this transformation, and that miracle took place when we least expected it, when we had nearly lost all hope.

It was Spring 1999, three years after Janice's murder, five years after the summer of death, and when my lawsuit was in the process of being settled. The kids were progressing through school and we were living an emotionless life. That's not to say that we weren't content, for there was even occasional laughter. After all, we had a lot to be thankful for: we and the children were healthy; we lived in a lovely home in a nice neighborhood; we were financially stable and, as a friend of mine once said to his spoiled children who were feeling sorry for themselves, no one was shooting at us. We had, in fact, stopped feeling sorry for ourselves, primarily out of guilt. True, we had experienced our share of ugliness, even lost a close family member to trauma, but one only had to watch the evening news to know that there were many more people facing tragedies just as bad or worse than ours. At some point, before a particular evening in the spring of 1999, we decided to move forward.

Pam and I spent a tremendous amount of time discussing our experiences, concentrating mainly on Janice. We analyzed her death over and over again, attempting to put it in some kind of perspective and move on. We tried going back to church, even involving ourselves in small group discussions, but to no avail. No one seemed to understand what we were going through, or perhaps we simply weren't able to clearly articulate what we were feeling. In any event, after we wallowed in confusion and depression for several years, we decided it was time to snap out of it and begin living life again.

What we didn't discuss much was the emptiness we both felt, even after our conscious decision to jump back into life. One thing Pam and I have always been able to do well is work. Give us a job, something to accomplish, something to keep us busy, and we are happy. Pam is one of those people for whom the expression was written, "If you want something done ask the busiest person." She is forever being asked to do things for school, church, the neighborhood association—you name it. She does all this and runs an active business. Pam's way of dealing with the emptiness was to fill it with jobs, commitments, and activities. It was only later that I realized that throughout all this activity she was walking around in a daze, a thinly veiled sadness that affected every aspect of her life.

Only her sense of duty pushed her forward. She was a rat in a maze with no direction, no context, just a labyrinth of obligation to walk. When one duty was fulfilled the next one presented itself. She longed to rise above this maze and see the big picture, to understand how she got to where she was so that she could navigate her escape.

I, on the other hand, am an overachiever. My greatest joy comes from my highest sense of purpose. It has always been this way for me. Clearly, my dark and brooding side was much more cultivated than Pam's. My compulsivity became my sanctuary, postponing brooding until all the work was done. Once my tasks were accomplished, it was time for sulking in solitude. It was during these periods that I tried to make sense of it all. I relived my experiences over and over in my head, compulsively recreating Janice's murder in my mind to the point of near obsession. I wondered what she felt: Did she feel pain, or fear, or perhaps the peace that I had heard described by so many just at the moment of death? I saw her face in the mirror, Jack creeping up behind her with the gun. Sometimes I tried to feel the horror she must have felt so that I could then figure out a way to replace it with something better, hoping that maybe she had been able to do the same thing. I was always left unsatisfied, empty, longing, lost.

We questioned the benevolence of God and felt overwhelmed by evil. I'm sure our children would attest that our over-protective-ness and paranoia reached an all-time high during this period. The funny thing about over-protection is that sometimes, at its root, is self-protection from further loss, sorrow, or pain. If further loss occurred, the possibility existed that we would lose ourselves forever.

It's sometimes hard to know when you have reached your low point until it has already passed. And sometimes it sneaks up on you. In our case it was a slow, smoldering descent into the depths of despair. Things just didn't seem as important as they once did. Exercise, once a staple of our daily lives, began to slip away. At first you find yourself excusing yourself every now and then, then for several days, then pretty soon you aren't exercising at all. Food becomes comfort, especially sweet, rich, high-calorie foods. Then you become less concerned about your appearance—a comfortable tee shirt becomes more desirable than being stylish or well groomed. Somewhere along the line you lose your patience with the children and their voices begin to grate on you, their incessant questions make you crazy. As you withdraw, they sense your disinterest and then become more testy, yearning to connect again, to feel loved again. But you have no love to give. You barely manage to get up each morning and only do so because they need you for their very survival.

One particular day I came home from the hospital a little earlier than usual. As I walked in I heard the TV blaring in the family room. Toys, games and schoolbooks were scattered everywhere. Opened bags of chips were on the sofa. The kitchen counter was so cluttered I couldn't find the surface. Yet no one was to be found. I went upstairs to the master bedroom. It was dark and the curtains were closed tightly as were the blinds beneath them. The TV was on, providing the only light in the room. Pam was in bed with the covers pulled up over her. On the bed were stacks of papers. I looked at the letterhead on one of them and saw that it was from the lawyer handling Janice's estate. The rest were bank statements, tax forms, and receipts. I tapped Pam lightly on the foot.

"Where are the kids?" I asked cautiously.

"In their rooms," she groaned from beneath the covers. "I couldn't stand them anymore."

"Oh…." Pangs of guilt and fear rushed through me. I was at work while she was at home, picking up the kids, feeding them, settling their squabbles, helping them with homework, all the while dealing with the aftermath of her dead sister's estate. There was absolutely nothing I could have said to make this situation better.

"Well, maybe I'll go see if they need anything…" I attempted.

"Fine, you go see if the little shits need anything. And, in the meantime, who sees what I need?" The covers were still pulled up over her head.

I slowly sat on the bed beside her, placing my hand on her side, gently stroking. Her body began to shudder beneath my touch. She drew a breath in such a way that I knew she was sobbing. There was nothing I could say, nothing I could do. Something had to break. I felt us on a spiral plummeting downward. For the first time, my intense personal fear morphed into fear for us both. Now, I was scared for us.

We were badly in need of a diversion. Fortunately for us, spring is the season for renewal, and in our world of major charities and private schools it was also the season for fundraisers. Our children's school was holding their annual auction, a combined social event and fundraiser. We had decided to attend because it was a chance to go out, get a babysitter, dress up, have a couple of drinks, talk, laugh, maybe even dance. It was a chance to be grownups and to feel alive. So we went.

Most of the evening was uneventful. We bid on a few items at the silent auction, items the kids had given us specific instructions about. We ate, drank, and even laughed. We enjoyed being with the people we knew from school, and mostly enjoyed having our minds occupied by something other than our own lives. To our immense relief, no one asked about Janice anymore or how we were doing. In fact, few actually knew. Some time ago we realized that people tend to shy away from those struck by tragedy, as if they are afraid of some invisible contagion, some evil that might rub off if they get too close. So we rarely talked about it much with anyone other than a very few close friends and family members. I never thought it would come up that night—after all, it had been years.

Then I ran into Sheree. Sheree Slone was the mother of one of the boys in my son's class and, at that point, simply an acquaintance. We had exchanged greetings in the school parking lot and at various functions. Our sons were in the same Cub Scout pack, so occasionally we ran into each other there. Pam had more contact with Sheree through various homeroom functions, but even so our interaction was extremely limited.

I don't remember the exact circumstances, but at one point during the evening I found myself face to face with her. Sheree is a petite woman with short, dark hair, pretty features, and an embracing smile complemented by a friendly, open nature. She has boundless energy which reveals itself the minute you meet her. That night there was a calmness about her, something that gave me a sense of peace. She asked me how I was, but unlike the previous times I was asked the same question that evening, she was sincere.

I answered positively at first, but her facial expressions begged for further explanation. So I simply said we were doing better, that we realized that one never gets over the premature, traumatic death of a loved one, that one simply learns to live with it, which was what we were doing. And then came her response: "You know, your wife needs to know that her sister is okay." She was intense, yet compassionately calm. Then she repeated it: "Janice is okay. She is in spirit, and she is at peace, and she would want you to know that she is okay."

I was at a loss to respond. Sheree's eyes were transfixed on mine, and her face was at total peace. We were suspended beyond anything external going on in that crowded, noisy room.

"Have you spoken to Pam?" I asked, hoping I didn't have to deal with this all by myself.

"Yes, we just spoke," she said warmly. "She told me the whole story about Janice. And I told her what I told you, that Janice is okay."

This came as a relief on several levels. First, I knew that Sheree hadn't known about Janice prior to that evening, and I would have hated to think that she could read my mind. I was, however, amazed that Pam had been so open and frank with her about it. She must have been as comforted by her effect as I had been. Secondly, I was relieved that Pam had heard what I had heard, because there was no way she would have believed me had she not directly heard it herself.

Something made me look off to my left, across the room. Pam was standing there by herself, a drink in her hand, with a blank expression on her face. She was staring at me. When our eyes met her mouth opened a bit as if she was about to say something. Instead she simply smiled. She nodded her head and then I cocked mine as if to ask a question. She nodded again. She had heard Sheree and she believed what she heard. Seeing her expression of peace I, too, believed.

At that moment our lives began to change forever. We had been led to the threshold of a new path in our life's journey. It was to be a path of questions and discovery, of faith and acceptance. Eventually our understanding would free us from fear and open us to love, which would lead to life. And it all happened because of a conversation, a coincidental meeting, or so it seemed. A teacher had appeared at the moment we were ready to learn.

CHAPTER FOURTEEN

Mercedes

Pam and I had very little to say to each other on the drive home that night. I think we were both afraid to admit that what Sheree had said captivated us because we wanted to maintain our skeptical position about her statements concerning the afterlife. By means beyond our comprehension, Sheree knew that Janice was not only okay, but that she wanted us to know so. Sheree's motive for sharing seemed pure enough: she had received information she was guided to convey to us and for which she would garner no personal gain. Even though her access to the other side of the veil shook us, her message also comforted us.

What I didn't find out until some time later was that Pam called Sheree the very next day. She prefaced her conversation with small talk about the fundraiser, the kids, and school matters. What she really wanted was to find out more about Sheree's revelations from the previous night. What did she know about Janice, and how could she find out more about her? So they talked. They talked a lot! Soon, they became friends.

Sheree felt she needed to share her own personal, intamate inner journey with Pam to help her understand. (My hope was that somewhere along the way they would take me along for the ride.) After they would meet, Pam would fill me in on the details of their conversations. She was like a young student, enthralled by everything new she was learning, unwilling to wait an extra minute to tell those she loved what she had learned. From these conversations, Sheree's story unfolded before me.

Up until the death of her dear grandmother, Mercedes, Sheree had led a storybook life. She was the only child of adoring parents. She had a private school education and a life filled with culture, depth, love and fullness. Her grandmother was an impactful presence in her childhood and remained so into adulthood. Sheree's parents were young, so her upbringing was shared by her vibrant, wise grandmother. Mercy was a confidante and guide. She was also a storyteller, and her stories always had a message, a lesson.

"You make your own destiny," Mercedes used to say, particularly during times when Sheree faced difficult decisions about school, career, and her love life. At times the young Sheree was frustrated by her grandmother's seemingly cryptic advice. By the time she herself became an adult, she understood and welcomed her grandmother's wisdom. As Mercy grew older, Sheree began to contemplate the possibility of losing her valued life-guide.

In the spring of 1994—interestingly the same year I faced so many deaths—Sheree's grandmother became terminally ill. After a rich and energetic life, this woman who had brought so much depth and texture to Sheree's life now faced her own death. Mercy lingered for many days in a near-death state before the decision was made to discontinue life support. Since Sheree was a nurse and therefore the health care adviser for the family, she became the individual upon whom that ultimate, painful decision rested.

During the days preceding the decision to take Mercy off life support, Sheree was with her constantly. When she was not physically present, Mercy remained at the forefront of her thoughts. Sheree was in turmoil. She had been raised Roman Catholic so had traditional Christian views about the soul and afterlife. She envisioned heaven as a place guarded by St. Peter, who stood atop majestic stairs just behind the pearly gates. Having never thought extensively about death, Sheree never had to integrate these concepts into her own life experience. Now that Mercy was leaving her, it didn't matter to Sheree where she would be "going"; the cause of such sorrow was that she was "leaving." Sheree simply could not deal with the reality of losing her grandmother.

 Sheree is an extremely sociable and gregarious person and, as a consequence, talked to everyone about her grandmother and her deepening despair about her imminent death. Her hairdresser had this advice for her: "Speak to your grandmother and ask her to contact you after she dies, to let you know that she is with you and that she is okay."

At first this sounded perfectly ridiculous to Sheree, so she dismissed her hairdresser's advice as foolish. But as Mercy's death approached she began to shift her opinion. A couple of days before Mercedes died, Sheree began to talk to her. She told her grandmother that she wanted the best for her, even if that meant discontinuing life support, but that she could not bear the thought of losing her. She instructed her grandmother to let her know from the "other side" that she was all right. Sheree was never sure if her grandmother understood what she was asking, but she repeated it over and over again, like a mantra, as she sat beside Mercy's hospital bed.

When Mercedes finally died Sheree was overcome with despondency. She did not know how her life would ever again have meaning without the tender guidance of her beloved grandmother. She went through the motions of the funeral—the mourning, the family, but she felt as if she herself was dead inside. Sheree had known intellectually that her grandmother would someday die, but she was too much a part of the fabric of her life to be prepared emotionally for it. Death didn't just mark the end of that part of Sheree's life, it was the end. Her grandmother was no more, and so was that part of her life which she had shared with this extraordinary woman.

As is so often true when someone intimately close to us dies, we also mourn the loss of that part of ourselves that connected us to the deceased. The more connected we are, the deeper the sense of loss. Certainly this was true for Sheree.

Approximately three days after Mercedes' death—in the afternoon following her funeral—Sheree felt so exhausted that she decided to lie down for a short nap. Her then-toddler son, who was also incredibly close to his great-grandmother, lay by her side. They both quickly fell into a deep sleep. Before long something startled Sheree, waking her from her slumber. Her attention was drawn to the ceiling, in the vicinity of the chandelier. In the dimness of the shaded light something began to take shape. It took on a reddish color and appeared to be shimmering, almost vibrating. It was translucent with wing-like structures at its sides, butterfly-like in appearance. It hovered there for quite some time, and then, as quickly as it appeared, it was gone.

This unexpected experience frightened Sheree. She concluded that it must have been a hallucination. Then recalling her bedside conversations with her grandmother—along with her direct request for Mercy to give a sign that she was okay—she wondered, could this be it? She had no way of knowing absolutely, and she was not yet ready to accept even the possibility that it could be. She tried to put the experience out of her mind, dismissing it as being due to exhaustion or grief.

Then, two months later, on the exact day of her grandmother's birthday, another strange event took place. That morning Sheree bought a can of coffee and placed it in its customary location in the pantry. When she went back to get it later that evening to make her husband some coffee, the can had disappeared! At first this seemed trivial. However, compulsive housekeeper that she was, Sheree always placed the coffee in exactly the same spot. Doubting herself rather than believing her eyes, she looked for it throughout the entire kitchen. She made her husband come into the kitchen and verify that the coffee can wasn't there. Tending to be less compulsive than Sheree, he passed it off simply as an oversight. Sheree, however, could not.

Sheree began reading about the spirit world in an effort to explore the afterlife. She didn't tell anyone, but her interest was prompted somewhat by the image she saw the day of her grandmother's funeral. She remembered that her grandmother loved coffee, particularly its aroma. Was the missing coffee a message from her grandmother? Was the red butterfly-like image also one?

Instead of being comforted by the possibility that her grandmother was trying to send her a message, she was frightened. While Sheree wanted desperately to know that her grandmother was still with her in some form, that possibility now scared her to death!

The next day the coffee can mysteriously reappeared in the pantry exactly where Sheree had placed it the day before. Her goose bumps morphed into a cold sweat. She ran to get her husband to show him what had happened. This time he too was convinced that something was indeed happening beyond their understanding.

Unexplainable occurrences began happening with increasing frequency. One day, while all alone in her home, Sheree heard a high-pitched squeaking sound that possessed an electronic quality, like an old-fashioned tape recorder fast forwarding. As she listened more intently, there were several different sounds interconnecting. She heard one, then the other, then the first again. Before long, she heard a third. They were "talking" to each other, cackling like hens. What were they? Who were they? Was her grandmother responsible for this, too?

She read and researched some more, seeking an answer to these unexplained incidents. She learned that those living in the spirit world do sometimes make contact with those living on the earth plane in just such ways as she was experiencing. She also discovered that the universe spoke to her in metaphors. For example, her research revealed that the red color she saw may have represented survival, and the butterfly-like image symbolized transition to another form in another dimension of life.

After praying so long for a way to make contact with her grandmother, Sheree began to realize that indeed she could.

Instead of welcoming this realization she simply couldn't handle it. She wanted her old life back, where death was death, life was life, and they didn't commingle! As she unfolded her story to Pam, she said that it was at this point that she simply shut down, stopped believing, stopped wanting to, and for a time stopped seeing.

Sheree always did what was expected of her, even as a child. She knew it was important to do well in school, to behave properly, to be a source of pride for her family. She followed the plan set forth for her generation: She completed college, found a husband, settled down, started a family, bought the right house in the right neighborhood, drove the right car, belonged to the right clubs, and associated with the right people. She was led to believe that by following this life prescription she would be happy forever after. Four years after her grandmother's death, Sheree began to realize that there had to be more. She was not happy, not fulfilled, and neither were many of her "right" associates. There was an emptiness inside that she couldn't explain and there existed a guilt about these feelings since she possessed all the trappings of life that a person could ever want. The hole that remained unfilled was caused by spiritual starvation, she discovered.

She simultaneously realized that she was living in a narrow world governed by fear, and that what God intended was for life to be motivated by love. She began to intuit that every individual is an integral part of the universe, and that the universe is part of every individual. She no longer denied this state of oneness, or ignored the unexplainable. Faith and acceptance are the keys that unlock the door to Truth, she learned. So her conscious journey began. She devoured the popular self-help books, ancient philosophy, the Holy Bible.

From her readings Sheree learned that there are three components to the self: physical, emotional and spiritual, and that this trinity must be in a state of constant balance if one is to live in harmony with the universe, with God. In an effort to improve and awaken the physical aspect of herself, Sheree began to work out with a trainer. He was not, however, your average health club trainer. He came from a Marine family and used this background as the basis for his training program. Naturally, discipline was the foundation of his training, for only in this way could goals be accomplished and self-confidence be gained. He took Sheree out in the central Florida heat to a public park she frequented as a child. He made her run the only hill in town, lift weights, and do calisthenics until she nearly dropped. He was not so much sculpting her body as he was challenging her spirit.

During her workouts, Sheree would share with her trainer about the metaphysical subjects she was studying. She shared with him the nature of the soul, its continuity with the universe, and its immortality. "You know, you don't die," she would say. The more she challenged him with these concepts the harder he seemed to make her work. "God is love and he is in all of us," she would say. "We are all one...." she would offer. He became visibly frustrated, which only spurred her on. As she gained confidence in the affirmations she gave to him, she also became physically stronger. The hill became her temple, a place where she pushed the physical aspect of herself, calmed her emotions, and fine-tuned her spirituality. She slowly but inexorably became an integrated person, more so I dare say, than any Marine he had ever trained!

As Pam listened to these stories she was absolutely enthralled. She had never met anyone so motivated to get to the bottom of the great questions of the universe, of human purpose. Pam's ethic of hard work in life was stronger than anyone's I know, so Sheree's heroic stories naturally impressed her. She became Sheree's devoted student and brought her lessons home for us both to share. And we discussed them at great length: Did I really think Sheree was visited by her grandmother? Did I believe that one's spirit could manifest itself from another dimension to the earth plane? Pam was always more traditionally religious than I, so it was easier for her to discuss the afterlife, how God handles those who lived lives he approved of, and the like.

I was skeptical of Sheree's stories—even somewhat cynical— about her interpretation of what she had "seen." The guiding principles of my life were the results of years of concrete medical and scientific training. So whether or not one believed in an afterlife didn't really matter. To us humans, life here on earth was the ultimate; it was all we could and did know about. It was this life that was sacred, this life that we tried our damnedest to preserve at all cost.

Surprisingly, I listened to Sheree's stories with increasing inter-est. Frankly, what intrigued me was the degree to which Pam was swept up by them. She was clearly moved, and what moved her was how changed Sheree seemed as a result of her experiences. Whether or not one believed the stories themselves, it was difficult not to believe their obvious effects. Sheree had arrived at an inner peace. Through her study, training, contemplation and understanding of her experiences, she achieved an understanding of life, the soul, and death. Pam described that when Sheree told these stories she seemed to be a woman from whose shoulders a giant weight had been lifted.

Sheree claims her awareness began with those Marine-like workouts, and described how, as she began to get into the best shape of her life, she felt a strength run through her—not merely a physical strength, but an emotional one. It was a strength that allowed her to put away fear and accept things she previously tried to ignore, deny, or run from. It was in those moments when she allowed things to be that her mind's eye opened and she began to intuit even more profoundly. She became aware of all that was around her including sensations and experiences. Soon after, she realized that there was no such thing as coincidence. Every person, every experience that came into her life was there for her to learn from, and it was her choice whether to accept or deny them. Denying was an act of fear; accepting was an act of love. And love was God's intention.

Sheree professed a lifelong love of birds. Since she was a child she picked up stray and wounded birds, nursed them back to health and sometimes raised their offspring. As she progressed through her spiritual study, she was thrilled to learn that birds metaphysically represent spiritual awakening, the ability of the soul to take flight, to transcend the earthly realm and soar closer to God. Because of this belief, feathers became spiritually significant to her, so much so that whenever she needed reassurance that she was following the right path, a feather would manifest.

On one particular day Sheree was driving her son and his cousin somewhere when she noticed a pigeon struggling alongside the road. Sheree stopped, scooped up the bird and placed it on the floor of her car. In that moment her son's plans were immediately changed! She stopped at a vet whose opinion it was that the pigeon had probably been hit by a car resulting in a broken wing. There was nothing he could do for the unfortunate bird, he said. As they spoke, the bird seemed to take a turn for the worse, manifesting internal injuries. Comforting the pigeon, Sheree made sure it did not feel alone, holding it as it peacefully died. She and the vet were so moved by the moment that they both wept. Later that evening Sheree was visited by her cousin, who was still troubled by the death of her father some years before. She asked to speak with Sheree because she had been experiencing strange feelings about him. She was somewhat conflicted about Sheree's claims that those who have passed on to the other side are able to contact dear ones remaining on the earth plane. During a contemplative moment in their discussion, Sheree felt very strongly that her cousin's father's spirit was present with them. She withheld saying anything so as not to frighten her cousin, but she did in fact see his image quickly pass by in the dining room mirror. What she did not know was that her cousin also saw the same image. In unspoken language they verified to each other what they had seen. The image then disappeared as quickly as it had come. Before they could begin to digest what they had experienced, there was a commotion near the entryway. They saw a pigeon wildly fluttering, batting its wings against the door's window. They rushed to the door, opened it, but the bird had vanished.

Sheree was convinced that the pigeon they heard and saw was the same one she had comforted earlier that day, that its spirit returned to thank her for allowing it to pass peacefully. That this occurred while simultaneously feeling the presence of her cousin's father was no coincidence. Coincidence is a phenomenon Sheree refers to as synchronicity, meaning that when simultaneous events occur (which on the surface appear unrelated) they are in fact contiguous.

One of the reasons why we have such a hard time understanding and accepting death, Sheree says, is because we understand and accept so little of life. What we don't understand—or more precisely what does not fit into what we think is our understanding of the universe—is coincidence.

One night Sheree and her husband were out to dinner with dear friends with whom Sheree felt comfortable discussing her experiences and their significance. This night as she shared with them, her friends told her that more people needed to hear and experience the comfort of her story. They encouraged her to write a book. As they spoke, she heard Van Morrison's "Moondance" playing in the background. "All the night's magic seems to whisper and hush," is a line from his song. It has always been a favorite of Sheree's, and mine. It is a celebration of life, love, dance, the night, the moon and October skies. It also has a mystical quality, a haunting magic…magic you can experience only if your heart is open to it.

Some days later as Sheree sat down to chronicle her experiences on tape, she turned on the radio. "Moondance" was playing.

The first night Sheree and I met to discuss ideas about her book we were at a coffee shop in Tampa. We sat at an outdoor table just as the sun was setting. Synchronicity made its presence known once again as "Moondance" began to fill the atmosphere. She was struck by the synchronicity.

CHAPTER FIFTEEN

Pam

Pam became one of Sheree's staunchest disciples. Sheree's optimistic convictions were infectious, even if some of her experiences seemed too "out there" to completely accept. It didn't bother my otherwise concrete-thinking wife that some of Sheree's notions challenged credulity. Since Janice's death, very little remaining in Pam's world made sense. What mattered now was that Sheree had found understanding and peace, both of which Pam yearned for.

I, on the other hand, had learned to live with the fact that I would never find peace. Accepting this reality gave me a perverse, cynical sort of peace. Life's purpose, I had decided, was to learn to deal with the shit that seemed to keep finding its way into one's life. I mimicked optimism for the sake of our kids, but that was where it ended. Soon enough, I opined, they would learn the truth about life's challenges. As easily as can be imagined, Pam's and my differing philosophies were beginning to strain our relationship.

One day—during the period when Pam and Sheree were spending so much time together—Pam suggested that she and I have lunch. I jumped at the opportunity. We considered it a real treat to spend an hour or so without the kids, enjoying the luxury of uninterrupted conversation. During these rare occasions, our conversation inevitably turned to the philosophical. This day was no different.

"I really like Sheree," Pam started.

"Well, I like her, too." (I'm a team player.)

"No, it's just that a lot of people think she is a little nuts. I mean you know how she tells everybody she meets about her bizarre experiences." Pam was rearranging her salad as she spoke, not making eye contact with me.

"That's why you're so great—so open-minded." Being free with compliments never hurt. Suddenly, I became unsure of where this conversation was going.

"What do you think?" She continued working with her salad.

"About what?" Of course I knew about what...I was just stalling.

"You know," she continued. "All this stuff with Sheree and everything."

"Well..." I set down my coffee cup trying to choose my words carefully. "I think it's great for her that she found you."

"Well, aren't you sweet!" she said in a mocking tone. "But you know that's not what I am talking about."

Of course I did. "Well, let me ask you." I thought for a moment. "What do you think about all this stuff? Do you believe she can see ghosts?"

"Come on, John." Pam was indignant. "She has never said she sees ghosts."

"You know what I mean—floating butterflies, coffee cans disappearing, dead birds and dead fathers appearing simultaneously. Seems a little woo-woo to me!"

"When you put it that way, of course—you and your cynical judgment." Pam was more defensive of Sheree than I expected. I'd better proceed with caution, I thought to myself.

"OK, fair enough." I mentally stepped back. "I was just trying to be funny—I'm not cynical!"

"Oh yes you are! All you doctors are." She carefully placed a dressing-soaked crouton in her mouth.

"Now, come on." I pretended to be offended. "That was uncalled for. I am as open-minded as the next guy."

"About some things, that's true." She was not taking my bait. She intended for this to be a serious conversation.

"So I guess I'm not open-minded about this, huh?"

"Not really. You can't accept the unexplainable. You can't even begin to believe that these things may have actually happened to Sheree."

I really didn't want to say anything that might hurt her feelings, but she kept pressing as if she really wanted to get into this with me. What did it matter what I thought? Why couldn't she just be happy knowing that it helped her…why drag me into this? "I have been very tolerant of all the time you have been spending talking to Sheree."

"Well, thank you very much for being so generous!"

"You know what I mean." I have a tendency to get whiny when I become defensive. Knowing how unbecoming this was to Pam, I tried to quickly let go of this behavior. "I know you need this, since Janice and all."

"Oh, you do, do you? You think I need this, huh?"

"Well, I thought you needed something to help you deal with it." I tried not to sound patronizing.

"Guess what I think?" She was staring straight at me now. (Both of us had stopped eating some time earlier). "I think you need something, just as much, if not more than I do."

I was flabbergasted. This was not a direction I thought our conversation would take. I was no longer sure where we were now headed. But I knew my wife, and if she thought I needed to go there she would take me, even if it meant dragging me and my resistance kicking and screaming. And so she began, and did not stop for another hour.

Pam agreed that Janice's death threw her for a loop. In fact, she said there was no question that she had been clinically depressed. The day she admitted to me that she had experienced fleeting thoughts of suicide was when her despondency over Janice's death had reached its depths. She confided that she rejected the idea because of me and the children. Not that we needed her, she said. (I immediately informed her of how wrong she was.) She then added that she didn't want to hit us with another loss, not on top of everything else.

Sheree came into Pam's life when she was at her lowest ebb. Pam admitted that while Sheree had some wild stories and incredible coincidences, Pam didn't care if they were true or not. What had affected her so profoundly was that Sheree knew they were true, and what they had taught her about life was even more powerful. It was these beliefs that allowed Sheree to rediscover her faith, a faith Pam felt we lacked in our lives. She told me that our problem—my problem—was that we were living a godless life, that we didn't believe in anything. She pointedly asked me if I believed in God.

I, of course, said yes, but then I hesitated. It had been so long since I really thought about it. What relevance did such a belief have in my life? Had I taken all my religious beliefs so for granted that they had become boilerplate ritual with no real meaning or application in my everyday life?

"You know, I became depressed after Janice died." She was so in control that I became envious. "But I think you have been depressed for years. You used to talk to me a lot more about the hospital, the ICU, your patients. Now there's barely a mention."

It was true. My so-called survival mode had reduced me to an emotional vacuum. I thought I was dealing with everything just fine. In truth, however, I had become an empty shell, just a robot going through the motions. Pam saw through me and she now considered it her assignment to get me to see through myself.

"The kids notice it, too, you know." Now she was hitting below the belt. "Your lack of emotion, your lack of passion. You don't have any fun with them. You feed them, take care of them, but you aren't really there. You're not really present. I think your treatment may be worse than the disease. You have emotionally lobotomized yourself. You can't stand to talk to Sheree because she challenges you. She challenges this wall you have built around yourself."

I remained speechless. This was torture. Had we not been at a restaurant with only one car I would have left her right then and there. I couldn't bear to hear any more.

"Call her crazy, but at least she has caused me to think." Pam was not going to stop now; she had me against the ropes. Was this what a twelve step intervention is like? "She has helped me to make peace with God again, to understand that there is so much more than just this sometimes miserable, seemingly incomprehensible life. We can't make sense of this life—all we can do is be open and try to understand. Closing down isn't going to get us anywhere, which is exactly where you are." She paused as I noticed a slight dampness around her eyes. "And I, for one, would like to get you back, the old you, the one who laughed, who had joy in his heart, who loved."

Wasn't this quite a switch? All this time, I thought it was she who needed help as she navigated the trauma of having lost her sister. In her mind, however, it was just the opposite. She was doing just fine! She had sought out someone who could help her, someone I had labeled as crazy. My unwillingness to learn from Sheree's experiences was of no service to me, or Pam.

"I thought I was just doing my job." I tried one last time to defend myself. "I know we have been through hell, but a lot of people go through a lot worse. Think about wars, accidents, terrorism! Survivors of those things do just that—they survive, they suck it up and go back to work. So that's what I've done. Yeah, I had a hard time with some of those deaths. The lawsuit about killed me, and then Janice died. But my way of handling it all was to get back to work, to take care of the hospital, of you, the kids, and eventually everything would be fine again. I was just doing my job." I couldn't bear to look up because I knew Pam was just shaking her head with that look of pitiful disappointment that drove me crazy.

"Yeah, well, guess what?" She took the napkin from her lap

and was getting ready to leave. Clearly, I was hopeless and she had enough of trying to get me to understand. "You really only have one job in this lifetime, and as far as I'm concerned, you're failing that miserably."

"What are you talking about!" I was struck by that one. This was going to degenerate into a true fight. Maybe that's why she was preparing to leave the restaurant.

"Your only job in this life, John, is to love…"

Just as I was preparing to crank our conversation up a few notches she simply stopped. She looked at the check that was sitting on the table, reached in her purse, pulled out some bills and left them on the little tray. She stood up, straightened herself, and began to walk away.

"I'm going to the potty, and then I'll meet you at the car. I'm driving." And with that she was gone.

Her use of the word "potty" was code. She really wasn't angry with me, it said, at least not to the point of no return. But she was definitely disappointed. I recalled the time when I backed myself into a corner during a poorly negotiated business deal, by not being assertive enough, and we ended up losing a lot of money. She was disappointed in me then, too. The next day, at work, when I opened up my briefcase there was a note from her: "I love you John Monaco, but you drive me crazy sometimes!"

"Potty" was the same sort of message. It was the word we used with our children, and as often happens when rearing children, it became part of our lexicon. To translate, Pam's use of that word meant that "we" were okay. I may not have been, but we were.

We had very little to say to each other for the rest of the day. Normally during such discussions, I used every technique I knew to keep the conversation going. Manipulation for sure, but sometimes it was all I had. It was when Pam became quiet that I knew hadn't a chance.

This time I lacked the energy or the will to rekindle the conversation. It had been too painful and cut me too close. I needed a break. Fortunately, I was off the rest of the afternoon. Before I picked up the kids from school I went for a long run while Pam retreated to the confines of her office. I introspected on the sea change in the basic dynamic of our family. I may have been the last one to feel it. As the rhythm of my running shoes hitting the pavement hypnotized me into a deep place within myself, it suddenly became very clear: I was now the one we were worried about. I was the one in trouble.

That afternoon I lost myself in the activities of running a household. Pam stayed in her office trying to catch up, which was often the case when I was not on call. I picked up some sort of take-out for us to eat during our individual shifts. I sat down with the kids while they ate, trying to go through the motions of asking them about school, their friends, and helping them with their homework. They seemed fine. Did they really feel that they weren't getting the full emotional commitment they deserved from their dad? I tried to detect it in their eyes, or in their laughter when I attempted to say something funny. I couldn't discern if they were missing anything. Perhaps they didn't know any better, I thought to myself.

Pam came to bed long after me. I had fallen asleep, but became roused a bit when I felt her presence. I remember thinking about the old adage that a couple should never go to bed mad, but I lacked the energy to fully awaken and speak to her. She was exhausted too, I rationalized to myself. Perhaps we would have some time in the morning, or I could call her after I got to the hospital. But not tonight, just not tonight.

I awakened to the smell of fresh coffee brewing, which was unusual since I was the one who usually made the coffee in the morning. It was early so the kids would not be up for another hour. I threw on shorts and a tee shirt and stumbled downstairs. The din of the morning news was in the background. Pam was sitting at the kitchen table with the morning paper in front of her, next to a mug of steaming coffee. Her hands were folded around the cup as if she was trying to warm them. I came from behind her so I couldn't see her face. If I could just see her expression, then I would be able to judge her mood, and then I would know what kind of a day we were going to have. I gambled anyway, and softly touched her shoulder as I went by.

"Good morning, baby," she said to me. It was so soft and sweet, that for a moment I wondered if we had made love during the night and I had forgotten about it!

"Hi, how are you?" I asked nervously.

As she turned to me I started. Amused, she chuckled under her breath. There was something different about her, a softness around the edges that hadn't been there before. It was the kind of haziness in which objects appeared before I realized that I needed glasses, except that this was more of a glow, almost a halo around her head and shoulders. It must have been the morning sunlight coming through the window, I concluded. But I couldn't stop staring. I knew she noticed, but she didn't say anything either.

"There was something I meant to tell you yesterday at lunch but we never got to it."

"You mean there was more?" I said sarcastically, assessing that she was in the mood to handle my sarcasm.

"Yes, wise guy, there was more. Stop worrying. I'm done attacking you!" We both laughed. The mood was decidedly lighter. I thought it might be a good day after all.

"Was it something about Sheree?" I tried to sound as open and as pleasant as I could.

"No, not really…." Pam's dramatic pauses were legendary. She took a sip of coffee, and continued. "She came to me…Janice…she came to me the other night in a dream. She looked beautiful, just like she used to look, only happier, more at peace, I think. She couldn't stop smiling. Her smile was always so beautiful, so infectious. Her arms were outstretched, kind of like, well, as if she was reaching for me. Jack was there, too, and they seemed all right together. He didn't speak, though, and remained in the background like he was ashamed or something. But Janice did speak. In my dream, John, she spoke directly to me. She said she was okay. She said I should stop worrying about her and go on with my life. She said she loved me, and then she was gone."

My jaw dropped; I know it did. I sat down at the table next to her and touched her forearm. Suddenly she threw both arms around my neck and buried her face in my chest. We both wept uncontrollably.

CHAPTER SIXTEEN

The Feather

Once the kids woke up, the comforting chaos of routine family life began to overtake us. We went about our duties as if nothing had taken place. I was not on call that morning, but had some administrative duties at the hospital. I would take the kids to school since Pam planned on tying herself to her desk. Since her dream, she told me, she had renewed vigor, less distractibility. She planned on taking advantage of this new-found productivity to finally catch up.

We kept catching each other in knowing glances and even giggled a few times. It was odd, like we were flirting in high school. I couldn't take my eyes off her. She was radiant. I swore she looked ten or fifteen years younger. When I told her so she laughed, tossed her head, and her hair flowed like it had when we first met.

After an uneventful trip to school with the kids I quickly disposed of my hospital duties and took myself out for coffee.

Sitting in the shade at an outdoor table, I pretended to read the sports page. Actually, I was people watching. I needed some time to ponder yesterday's lunch, Pam's dream and its significance. What really had me going was the new person she had become, nearly overnight.

I no sooner sat down at the wrought iron table and chairs when I noticed a familiar silhouette walking up the sidewalk: it was Sheree. She had already seen me by the time I had spotted her and she headed straight in my direction. As she got closer she smiled but her expression contained something else, concern perhaps. I motioned for her to join me.

"Coffee?" I asked, trying to lighten what seemed to be a portentous moment.

"No thanks, John. I've only got a minute…got to be some-place." She slid her petite body into the seat. She was clearly preoccupied. "You know, I never wanted all this to happen."

I was puzzled and decided not to respond. Then clarity entered and I asked, "You spoke to Pam, didn't you?"

She continued without directly answering the question. I knew immediately that they had spoken. " All this spirit stuff…you know I never asked for it. All I ever wanted to do was hear from my grandmother…to know she was okay. In fact, when I first started getting all these messages, it drove me crazy. I thought about jumping off the highest building!"

Sheree was capable of long, uninterrupted dialogue, so I decided not to interrupt her. Yet, as she spoke, she lapsed into that peaceful person I had come to know. I think she had been nervous when she first sat down. Pam and she had definitely spoken and Sheree was here to defend herself. Ironic, actually, since I wished I could feel the way she felt, perhaps even see what she has seen.

"Let me tell you what happened to me one time. One of my old childhood friend's father had not been feeling well. And I had been having dreams about him. I was even having strange feelings about him during the day. Then, one day it had been particularly strong. He was going to die. I knew it! So I called her, and I said, 'How's your Dad?' And she said, 'Fine. He was just feeling a little dizzy this morning so was thinking about going in for some tests.' I asked her to just trust me and go with him. She did, and he was fine. I think they even laughed about what I had told her. I'm sure she thought I was an idiot. But then later that night, he took a turn for the worse. They found out he had a huge abdominal aortic aneurysm which had been slowly leaking, which is why he had had the dizzy spells. That night, the aneurysm burst and he died."

"My God."

"You're telling me! That's what I mean. I wish I never even had those feelings. My only comfort is that my friend got to spend time with her Dad before he passed away, otherwise she might not have."

"So maybe that is your role." Was I actually now comforting Sheree?

"Maybe, but you have to understand. This happens to me all the time, so I've just resigned myself to it. I wanted to be in tune with the universe, and now I've received what I asked for. I surrendered, now that I'm aware that I am to use my life for doing good. But understand: I don't care if you believe all my stories. Sure, I hope that you don't think of me as crazy, but believe what you like about my experiences."

She had a purpose, there was no doubt. And I was beginning to feel a bit uncomfortable, like she had been reading my mind or something. Sheree continued, "There is something you have to believe, though; that is all I ask. You have to believe that our souls go on after us, into eternity. You must believe this. You must have faith."

She was looking past me at this point, into another realm, another reality.

Then, as if a wave passed over her, she was back to her self and settled back into a more peaceful mode again. I guess she just needed to get that off her chest. Maybe she was afraid that I thought she had stolen Pam's psyche. Really, I wanted to thank her. And then ask her if she could help me!

"Let me tell you one more story." I couldn't help but smile, and so did she. "Do you know Mrs. Huntley, the third grade teacher at the school?"

"Yeah, sure, she taught Elizabeth," I responded.

"Well, we never got along so great when my son was in her class. I always found her a little cool, but I was wrong about that." Sheree's endearing smile returned. "When I told her some time back about my experience with birds and feathers—especially about the symbology of white pigeons and purity and the soul's flight back home—she didn't seem very much interested in my sharing. Anyway, we were standing near each other at assembly, and out of the blue she says, 'I must talk to you. If you have time after school give me a call. My husband has cancer.' In the next instant, I found myself saying,

'Yes, and they haven't given him much time to live!' Her jaw dropped, and mine nearly did too. So when I called her, she shared this beautiful story of what unfolded prior to her husband's death.

"One night their son went out to pick them something up for dinner. When he returned to his car, a pigeon came out of nowhere and flew right into the car window. He couldn't get it out! Every time he tried, the bird successfully evaded him. So he finally gave up, got in the car…"

"With the bird?" I asked.

"Yes, with the pigeon. And the amazing thing was that the pigeon sat on his shoulder all the way home. And then, when he got out of the car, it stayed on his shoulder. By the way, it was a white pigeon, and when they got in the house, it flew off her son's shoulder, out to the porch and onto her husband's shoulder, and there it stayed."

"And they couldn't get rid of it."

"They didn't really try. They placed it in a cage, but most of the time it just sat there on his shoulder. And he loved it!"

"Amazing." I really was dumbfounded.

After Sheree left, I just sat there for a while, sipping at my coffee which had long turned cold. I was glad I had nothing pressing to do because I needed some time to think. Lately, I hadn't allowed myself much time to just be. (I didn't especially like being alone with my thoughts. I was much happier when I was busy doing my job.)

Since it was a lovely day, I decided to take a walk along a quiet, shaded street where I could lose myself for a while. Something about the cool breezes and the warm sun freed my imagination. I let my mind wander. It had been so long since I let myself enjoy really feeling alive.

Thoughts began flying in at a rapid pace. I saw images, like an internal slide show. I remembered Alex, and Karen, and Alexis, followed by all the patients from the past. I saw Pam's face, the one I had seen earlier this morning, the glow it had, the peace and joy. I saw my children's faces and my heart ached—not out of sadness, but with an ache caused by pure joy.

Far down the straight, tree-lined street, in the distance, I saw the image of someone coming toward me. It was a jogger, but the person was still far enough away that I couldn't even make out the sex. I stared. The rhythmic nature of the strides was comforting, my head may have even bobbed with the beat as I watched. As she got closer I could see a ponytail swinging back and forth with each stride. Her arms were held up high, elbows flexed, overflexed really, with fists loosely clenched. This triggered a memory of the time we went to watch Janice take part in the Triathlon in Panama City, and how beautiful her stride was. (Janice had finished first female in her age group. We still had her trophy, which Pam took out and dusted from time to time.)

As I began to make out more of her appearance, I saw that the jogger had the same strawberry blonde hair, the lean, muscular legs, rippling arm muscles. She had on a cut-off tee shirt. When the jogger was less than a block from me, I could see that she was smiling. I have always been amazed by people who can smile while they run. To love an activity that much, to have that much joy, the way Janice used to. Could it be....

For a split second something pulled me from my thoughts. Meanwhile, the jogger turned up a side street. I ran to the corner, trying to get a closer glimpse, but she was too fast, much faster than I. She was nowhere to be seen. I wanted to get a closer look.

I wanted nothing more in the world at that moment than to see her again.

I stopped at the corner and leaned up against a tree, staring down the channel out to the open bay. The sunlight glittered on the rippling water. The breezes blew my hair. I was exhausted. I wanted to lie under the tree and take a nap. I wanted my mind to go back to where it had been a few minutes earlier…to the peace and joy I sensed. I wanted to see that jogger again.

As I turned back in the direction of the coffee shop, something caught my eye: it was a fluttering movement in the air just above me to the left. It was a feather, perfectly formed and pristine, which must have just fallen from a bird passing overhead. I watched it swing back and forth in the breeze, slowly descending to the ground. Something told me to let it float, to let it finish its journey. Eventually it did, settling itself precisely on my shoe, as if it were going to continue its journey with me. I still have that feather today.

CHAPTER SEVENTEEN

Love

Several weeks ago, I took care of a critically ill thirteen-year-old. His illness began two weeks prior when he sustained an injury to the tip of his finger in the form of a small cut. The wound was not cleaned or cared for, and so it became infected. In response, one of the lymph nodes in his armpit also became inflamed and infected.

He was brought to the emergency room when infection became so severe that the bacteria had begun to proliferate in his bloodstream, releasing toxins as it traveled. He was found in his bed at home, where he had gone after vomiting and feeling poorly all day. He was completely unresponsive. Except for occasional shaking movements which were at first thought to be seizures, he could not move.

By the time I saw him, in our PICU, his blood pressure and respiratory status had stabilized somewhat, but he remained stuporous. His only response was to deep, painful stimuli, and even then he responded only by groaning and moving his head slightly from side to side. He was severely impaired neurologically, and remained that way even as his other systems showed signs of improvement. This worried me. Had he sustained a stroke, or some other brain insult? Did he have an unusual encephalopathy that we had not yet diagnosed? Was there more going on here than we had, at first, realized? Only time and diligent bedside management would answer these questions.

That was what I told this boy's parents as we discussed his case, at the bedside in the PICU at three o'clock in the morning. They were very distraught. Their family had been hit with several catastrophes in a short period of time, and they weren't sure if they could handle something bad happening to their son. I told them to be hopeful, that we were doing everything we could, that he was already showing signs of improvement, which they should consider encouraging news. I shook their hands and let them know that I was only a phone call away if anything were to happen, and they seemed comforted by that. And then, as I had done hundreds of times before, when I felt that they had been sufficiently updated, I turned to leave the unit.

Something, however, made me change my mind. I turned and looked back at the boy's parents. They stood huddled around his bedside. His mother stroked his hair while whispering continually in his ear. His father was closer to the foot of the bed, with one hand on his wife's back, caressing it slowly, while he held his son's hand with the other. I walked back toward the bed, smiled at these wonderful people. They looked up at me. I then proceeded to pull up a chair. I sat down across from them, made myself comfortable, watched and listened. I checked on them several times, long into the night, until the light of the morning sky began to filter through the PICU window. We talked about their son—not just about his illness, or his chances of recovery, or the distinct possibility of his dying—but about him. They told me about his early childhood, about how good his grades were in school, how much he enjoyed video games and going fishing with his grandpa. They told me how awful his diet was, how he would choose McDonald's French fries over just about anything else. We laughed, and occasionally shed a tear together. And with me sitting there with them, they told that boy over and over again how much they loved him. I wanted to tell him too, but no matter how hard I tried, I couldn't. Not yet. Someday soon, I said to myself, I will.

CHAPTER EIGHTEEN

Lee

I have a friend—I should say I had a friend—who passed away several weeks ago. Lee was one of the most courageous and remarkable people I have ever known. He was quadriplegic, having sustained a spinal cord injury in his late teens in a rodeo accident. In his late fifties when he died, he spent the last several years in and out of the hospital as the complications of being wheelchair bound all those years had begun to catch up with him.

The spring before his passing, Lee suffered a respiratory arrest: he "died," as he liked to tell everyone, and during the resuscitation was placed on a ventilator and sent to the intensive care unit. Due to many factors—but mainly because the pulmonologists felt that his respiratory muscle strength would not sustain him off the ventilator—it looked as if the end had arrived. He did not want to live the rest of his life on a breathing machine, and he and his wife agreed that the endotracheal tube should be removed and the ventilator turned off, so that nature would be allowed to gracefully take its course.

My friend was not a religious man, and made it very clear that he did not believe in an afterlife. In fact, after his "dying" episode last spring he sarcastically wrote everyone to tell them that he had not seen a bright light, he did not feel himself float above his body nor had he seen any virgins. He had that kind of sense of humor.

But he was scared. In fact, several days before he knew that the tube would be pulled and that he would most certainly die, he asked to see me. We had had several previous discussions about death. One in particular was prompted by my telling him of my desire to write this book. We agreed upon the notion that modern American culture had not yet faced up to the inevitability of death, nor do contemporary people consider death as part of the circle of life. Even though he did not accept any theories—religious or otherwise—of what happens to us after death, he felt very strongly that death was part of the process of life, and that it was a component of the process that we as a culture had tried very hard to deny, ignore, and escape.

Over the years I told him that I had seen far too much death, but that it eventually became easier for me to deal with because I came to truly believe that there is more after this life. I described how I felt that modern religion had done the best it could with the subject, but that what happens to us afterward is probably impossible for us to comprehend given any paradigm we understand in life. He accepted this hesitantly, opining that it was quite flimsy philosophically.

I went on to tell him that there is one thing that I am sure of: the entire purpose behind human existence is love, and whatever happens to us after this life includes unconditional love. I went on to share how I had been overcome by just such feelings of love, several times in my life, at the bedsides of dying children and their families. It was these experiences, these miracles of death as I had come to call them, that had convinced me that there was so much more to life, and to life after death, that we could not possibly understand during this lifetime. And that was where faith came in: faith is the bridge that connects our hearts to that which cannot be rationally explained, I offered to him.

Lee indulged me and promised he would think about what I had to say. He thanked me for the opportunity to discuss these painful subjects, and I told him I was glad to do it.

Remember, these conversations took place while my friend was still on the ventilator. This meant that he had a plastic tube placed in his mouth, between his vocal cords, down his trachea and into his lungs. It is impossible to speak when one is on a ventilator. Therefore, all of our conversation took place with my speaking and his writing on a legal pad.

Then we embraced, I told him that I loved him, and made him promise to think about our conversation. I hoped that he would, but I knew he was stubborn and possessed a certain healthy cynicism, which made me uncertain.

The next day on my way to the pediatric ward, I stopped by the ICU to check on my friend. I paused at the nurses' station as I entered the unit, where they informed me that he had enjoyed a very restful night. This surprised me a bit as I thought he might have been restless after the conversation we had.

Lee's bed was across the unit, and he spotted me the moment I walked in. As I approached him I noticed that he was sitting up in bed, an unusual position for a ventilated patient. His endotracheal tube was hanging from his lips and appeared completely out of place, and more than a little absurd. As I looked at the smile on his face and the sparkle in his eyes he exhibited the biggest grin I had ever seen. His frail arms were open at about chest height, as far as he could raise them. In his hand he held a clipboard with a legal pad. He held it up for me to read as I entered the room. On it were written the following words that I shall never forget…"Thanks, I am ready…"

The words weren't really necessary, as I could see from the joy in his face that indeed he was ready.

AFTERWORD

by Sheree Slone, RN

⋅—⋅ ☰✦☷ ⋅—⋅

$\mathbf{M}$y introduction to the spiritual realm was by a rude and suspect teacher: Death. Not just death in general, but in particular when, in 1994, my beloved grandmother Mercedes transitioned to the next dimension of life. Prior to my face-to-face encounter with this great mystery we call death, I had no curiosity about the existence of any invisible, spiritual dimensions of reality unknowable by the five senses. Simmering in the juiciness of life as a nurse, wife and mother drowned out any inclination to actively seek answers to deeper mysteries.

All of that began to morph before my very eyes as I sat at my beloved grandmother's bedside while she lay in a coma, awaiting release from a physical body ravaged by the burden of its essential functions shutting down. The day before Mercedes made her transition, I gasped in awe as I witnessed her facial features shape-shift from those of an elderly, dying woman of 83 into an appearance of freshness, a beauty in total contradiction of the facts of her physical condition. Of course I kept my experience to myself, lest I be accused of having an overactive imagination due to grief, or of being unwilling to let go of this woman who was a giver of unconditional love throughout my life. Imagine my relief when family and well wishers who came to pay their respects commented on the extraordinarily increasing glow of incredible beauty upon her face.

While I could claim no absolute knowledge of what happens to an individual after death, nor provide factual evidence of the existence of an afterlife, my love for my grandmother birthed a fervent hope that what I had been taught as a child about the heavenly realm was indeed accurate. I suspected that I was romanticizing when I considered the possibility that her face was radiating an anticipatory joy of reuniting with her beloved husband of 24 years, Jack, my grandfather, who died unexpectedly in 1955. (He rolled over in their bed, told her goodnight and instantly left his body.) Or is it possible that she was already—prior to leaving her body—aware of his presence? It seemed the higher part of wisdom to simply leave all possibilities open, mostly because I wanted her heart's desire—whatever that might have been—to be fulfilled. She had earned my trust in life, so it was easy for me to extend it as she approached death.

I was not prepared for the events that followed her passing, beginning with how I missed the sound of her voice and the soft touch of her comforting hand—all the more meaningful now that her physical presence has gone. I ached for her wise counsel which, when I adhered to it, often changed the course of my life. To me, Mercedes was not only all-loving, she was all-powerful. And it was precisely this that convinced me that she possessed the ability to "give me a sign" of the continuum of existence. With the faith of a child I was sure that her love for her family would traverse universes to share the cosmic knowledge she now possessed. And so, equipped with an open heart and an open—though occasionally vacillating—mind, I waited.

There is no way to describe the paradox of fear and comfort I experienced when only three days after Mercedes' transition, signs indeed began to manifest in my life. I was joyous, but confused, because I had no frame of reference for what was happening. This set me on a course of research and study of the possible existence of other dimensions of reality, the eternality of the soul, and the chasm that seems to lie between our three-dimensional world and the fourth, fifth ad infinitum. I learned that whatever the human mind can conceive or define, the limitlessness of the Ineffable is far greater.

But back to my chronology. Soon, after making direct connection with Mercedes, I somehow once again felt uncomfortable about my newly-found ability to commune with her. So I asked her to stop, as though she was the root cause of my experiences. She obediently complied. But by 1998 I could no longer ignore or endure the suffering caused by the void of her presence in my life. Nevertheless, I summoned the discipline to rise above any temptation to give in. The price of this denial was expensive. I shut down my intuitive awareness and functioned in the claustrophobic world of empirical evidence.

Gently, the gossamer veil separating this realm from the next began once again to disintegrate, opening deeper gateways into the unseen. Let me assure you at this juncture that I was not then nor am I now a "woo-woo" kind of individual. Simply, most organically my mind's inner eye began to open, my spiritual journey claimed a firm foothold in my life, and I could no longer deny the intuitive awareness that sees what is unseen by the human eye. Doubts, denials, fears and confusion were replaced by the simplicity of a consciousness that knows and humbly accepts what it knows through grace. More and more I consciously realized that all beings are a part of this invisible spiritual blueprint, interconnected parts of a cosmic design, equally candidates for enlightenment.

Synchronicity then became my daily experience, and I lived in cadence with a universal rhythm that inspired my utmost trust in allowing it to guide the course of my life, and entrust to it the perfect unfoldment of the lives of others. So there was no cause for awkwardness when in the spring of 1999, at my son's school fundraiser, I approached Pam Monaco who also had a son in the same class.

Following our polite greeting out of my mouth came, "I want you to know that there is no death—people don't die." I had no foreknowledge that she was recovering from a family tragedy and subsequent trauma. I simply obeyed an intuitive urging to share with her that life does not end with death, that there is a rebirthing into another dynamic dimension of life. This simple, earthly proclamation loaded with eternal implications brought a flood of relief to her, evaporating any discomfort my seeming forwardness might have at first caused. I should add that I also met Dr. John Monaco, Pam's husband, that same evening. Though he did not participate in my initial conversation with Pam, nevertheless a meaningful connection was made.

After some time of cultivating my friendship with Pam, John and I also began to open-heartedly share our joys, disappointments, insights, doubts and convictions about life's seeming mysteries. Our respective experiences with the death of loved ones, as well as John's experience as a pediatrician, fueled our desire to provide the comforting knowledge that there is no separation between souls, not in this realm or any other. Our willingness to be spiritually, mentally and emotionally vulnerable led to our partnership in writing *Moondance to Eternity* with the heartfelt hope that it will be of service to our human family with whom we share the common experience of living, of our loved ones dying, and ultimately our own exit from this three-dimensional universe. May joy, trust, compassion, curiosity, peace and love accompany you every step of the way.

– Sheree Slone, RN
Tampa, Florida

The Moondance of Your Life

Years have now passed since my night with Felix, the baby who died in his parents' arms the very first night of my pediatric residency. When I think back over all the years, all the patients and all the life that has passed since then, I sometimes feel as if I have learned a great deal. Then, other times, I feel as if there is still a tremendous amount to learn.

My own children are now teenagers. Pam and I are slipping into late middle age and trying to do so as gracefully as possible. There are challenges ahead of us, perhaps as trying and painful as the ones behind us. And there will inevitably be difficult times. There will be sorrow and loss, just as certainly as there will be joy and triumph. That is the nature of this life on earth. That, indeed, is the human condition. It is this condition that we must accept if we are to find any peace whatsoever. To accept this condition we must have a strategy, and a philosophy with which we can approach life. We gain these tools from what we learn from past experiences. It is my hope that some of these tools can also be learned from the experiences of others. My wish is that you, the reader, can glean some of these tools from my experiences.

The stories of people's lives presented here have changed me, and hopefully just by reading them they have changed you. What I hope is that they have made you better, stronger and more able to cope with whatever heads your way, from the most unexpected tragedy to the most joyous triumph. Each person will undoubtedly react to what has been presented here in different ways. There are some major themes, however, that hopefully all will recognize and accept:

LIFE IS ETERNAL

This is perhaps the most important lesson, and from it all others will follow. It seems simple: the thought that there is something more after this life. In fact, when asked, most people will tell you that they believe there is something after this life. Virtually every religion has as a major tenet the belief in an afterlife. Even many agnostics and atheists will admit, when pressed on the subject, that they wonder if there is something more. Yet most of us are so caught up in the details of our everyday lives that it is often all too easy to forget that this life is brief and transitory.

What I hope you will take away from *Moondance to Eternity* is a restoration of the faith you probably already have: faith that the soul is eternal and life on this earth is simply one phase of our eternal journey. There can never be absolute scientific proof of this. And it is not offered here. What is offered is the suggestion that no other explanation is plausible.

But if we accept the notion that this life is just a phase, a stage in the whole journey of eternity, our view of life changes. I believe this is a gradual process. It may take years or it may even take a lifetime. But sometime during this life, it is essential that we come to grips with this concept. And once we do, everything changes. We will be able, after completely accepting the concept of eternity, to view this life as a step along the way, a time for education and improvement as we prepare ourselves for the rest of the journey. Whether you embrace the Judeo-Christian concept of Heaven and Hell or the Buddhist concept of Karma and reincarnation, the way we approach this life on earth is the same. It becomes our mission to become better people, to live in service to those around us, to give ourselves to those we love and those in need.

Once we accept the concept that life is eternal, then our view of death changes as well. It is no longer an ending, but a transition, from one stage of eternal life to the next. Since it is not a finite ending the next major concept must be true.

DEATH MUST NOT BE FEARED
This is a tough one and seems counterintuitive. Everything we learn in secular life, medicine, and science,

teaches us that death is the ultimate enemy…the thing that must be avoided at all cost. If we have the faith to believe that life is eternal, then it is only natural to reject the finality of death. If it is not final, and if it is only a transition, then it is not to be feared. We may fear the manner in which we will die—whether or not there will be pain or suffering. And we may fear being separated from those we love in this world. This is perfectly understandable. But we must not fear that in death, our lives will end forever. If we accept that in death, our soul will simply pass from one stage of eternal life to the next, then death will inevitably appear different to us. Instead of the gloomy and horrific ending we have been programmed to expect, death will become for us the moment when eternity declares itself to us.

Accepting this allows us to view the miracle of life in a more cyclical way. We all view childbirth as a miracle and it indeed is. But, in reality it is simply a passage from one form of life to another. In the same way, we can begin to view death as a miraculous passage from one eternal life form to the next. I would not feel so sure of this if I did not view so many of these miracles, outlined in the preceding pages, with my own eyes. So many times, once the inevitability of death is accepted by patients and then their loved ones, there is a moment of peace, even joy. That peace and joy reflect our own innate knowledge that the miraculous passage is about to take place. It will be so much easier to grieve the loss of our loved ones once we can finally accept the miracle of death.

MIRACLES ARE EVERYWHERE, AROUND US EVERY DAY

The challenge is to notice. Feathers are a wonderful reminder of this. They are always there, on the ground, wherever there are birds flying above. Yet, how rarely we see them. But if we force ourselves to pay attention, even actively seek them out, they will suddenly begin to appear everywhere. Try it. And once you have collected all the feathers you could possibly ever want, extend this notion to the rest of your lives. Take a moment, wherever you go, to observe the details of life all around you. Absorb the sights, smell the smells. Listen to the sounds. You may hear your own Moondance without even realizing it is playing! Give thanks for the blessings around you constantly. Let that be your daily mantra. The joy you feel will be immeasurable. And eternity will be even easier to accept. The miracle of eternal life will come naturally when the miracles of daily life are appreciated.

CHILDREN ARE A TREASURED SOURCE OF WISDOM

This seems cliché to many, and in its shallowest form it is. By getting to know children, really know them, the depth of their wonder will become even clearer to you. It is our job, as adults, to teach them about life. Yet often our own concept of life is distracted by the demands of everyday living. We begin to think of our lives in terms of careers, deadlines, goals and relationships. These are important, of course, but they are not the essence of life. They are simply preoccupations.

Children view life in its purest form. What they seek most is love, and what they seek most to give, is love. The older they become, the more clouded this motivation becomes. But deep within all of us, it is still there, longing to be expressed. The innocent laughter of children compared to the restrained, careful laughter of adults demonstrates the fundamental difference between the two.

Let the children be our teachers whenever possible. How many times in the preceding pages did the child teach the parent how to deal with tragedy? We saw children comforting adults and, in fact, giving them permission to "let go". While it is true that we have the responsibility to protect them and to teach them about the harsh realities of this life, perhaps we should open our minds and our hearts to what children have to teach us—lessons that can only be fully understood at the beginning and at the end of life, when its realities are clearest.

LIFE MUST BE LIVED WITHOUT FEAR

We have discussed that once we understand that death is a transition, and not an ending, we will no longer fear it. By extension, once we can live life without fearing death, many of our other fears will dissolve as well. Fear that is chased from life will be replaced by joy and love. This will then open us up to new experiences that will result in greater growth and deeper understanding. We will see the decisions in our life with much better clarity, and treat the people in our lives with more compassion and

acceptance. Everything in our lives will be seen in a more
positive light.

SERVING OTHERS CULTIVATES LOVE

Many people work in service industries, such as medicine
or nursing, yet they have never fully embraced the concept
of service. To do so, the above concepts must also be
embraced. Only after fear is replaced by love, the concept
of eternal life is accepted, and death is confronted and
accepted as the transition it is, can we truly live in service
to others. Once we see that the higher purpose of our lives
is to live in the service of others, only then will we truly
feel joy. Only then will we have rediscovered the love that
every child possesses and expresses freely.

If *Moondance to Eternity* only opens a window into your
mind, then it has accomplished something. Once you have made
the conscious decision to live your life free from the fear of death,
then you have truly succeeded. I wish you luck on your journey,
as I hope you wish me in mine.